STUCK
IN MY OWN
FAMILY TREE

STUCK
IN MY OWN
FAMILY TREE

by

PATRICIA WEBSTER STEWART

Stuck In My Own Family Tree
© 2007 by Patricia Webster Stewart
Cover illustration by J. N. Stewart

First Edition, published 2007
First printing paperback edition September 2007
Printed in the United States of America

Library of Congress Control Number: 2007907017

ISBN: 978-0-6151-5913-3
PUBLISHED BY PATRICIA WEBSTER STEWART
Taylors, South Carolina
www.patriciawebsterstewart.com

Buy This Book
www.lulu.com/content/1061912

To my son Stewart in memory of your grandma Pat Stewart. She had a deep love of reading and family.

2021

To Jack, who encouraged me, edited my work, kept the publisher straight and made this book happen.

and

To my seven children, mother, father, sisters, grandmothers, aunts, uncles and cousins who populate my family tree. They made these stories come true.

Preface

Do you sometimes wonder where you fit in, especially when you look around at a family reunion or a big family occasion like a wedding or funeral? Who are these goofy people? Am I really a relative of that clown over there making a fool of himself?

After I married my husband Jack and had seven children, I realized we were creating the next generation of family characters. These children brought spouses into the mixture and eventually brought grandchildren, another generation of characters.

I began writing stories when my seventh grade teacher gave us the assignment to write a "composition." I loved doing this and it set me up as a writer.

As the years went on, I kept writing as a form of escape from the daily confusion and chaos of life with seven children. They provided an endless source of material. The children moved on to college, marriage and careers. This gave me more time to write.

While the children were still at home I struggled with a typewriter. Later I entered the computer age, happy to give up that hated typewriter. I barely passed the typing class I took in high school. The computer proved to be my passport to putting out a decent manuscript that I could submit.

I listened to stories of a Grossmutter who threw her dead leg under a hospital bed. This story prevails after some seventy years.

My sisters and I got in trouble for telling the neighbors that we were still hungry one evening when my parents had a dinner party and fed us early.

My sister refused to go to first grade for several weeks while Mom literally dragged her to school.

A cousin ran away from home, from Father Flanagan's Boys' Town, and became a World War II hero.

Another cousin had an exciting time delivering her first child. She gave birth to a daughter on the Autobahn in Germany.

I married into a family that has an equal amount of curious history. Jack's grandmother Stewart came from a most complicated genealogy. She came from a family with several siblings. After her father died, her mother married a widower with more children. These two people had several more children, making a maze of whole, half and step-siblings. Jack had a hard time remembering where his mysterious Aunt Bessie fit into his family tree. As I read the genealogy, I too had a difficult time with the intertwining branches. And any time anyone mentioned Aunt Bessie, it was always in a whisper so the children and neighbors couldn't hear.

Melanie, my daughter-in-law, gave me a pillow with the following message on it: "My family tree is full of nuts." That pretty well sums up what I have to say in this book. They may be nuts, but they are *my* nuts!

Acknowledgements

Thanks to the members of the South Carolina Writers Workshop, Greenville Chapter. They gave me encouragement, hope and thoughtful insights into my work, enthusiastic support and candid advice.

Thanks also to June and Joe for their critical comments that helped polish this finished product.

Contents

Preface

Grossmutter's Legacy   1

Aunt Marie, AKA Rosie the Riveter   3

Aunt Cecilia's Honeymoon   6

My Family's Greatest Hero   9

Memorial Day 1945   11

Stephanie's Journey   14

Remembering the Dinner Party   23

Cherries and Arthritis   27

Mary Ann and Me   31

Grandma Webster's Chocolate Chip Cookies   34

Whatever Happened to Baby Chick?   37

What My Father Taught Me   39

Kelly's Special Delivery   44

The Sound of Silence   49

Three Dog Night in Concert   53

What Shall I Do With the Palms?   55

The Longest Toe   66

Finding Michele   68

New Life Phases   70

Sentimental Memory Books   74

I Would Never Do That!   77

The Circle of Life   80

Helen, Rebel without a Cause   83

Voting in 2004   87

The Songs of My Life   90

Jack's Stories   93

Opposites Attract   107

About the Author   109

Grossmutter's Legacy

Grossmutter frowns in almost all the faded photos of her. Perhaps it is because she had no teeth. I never knew Grossmutter because she died before I was born. All I have are the photos my mother passed on to me. She is my great-grandmother, Theresia Fiedler, born in 1838.

Grossmutter's birthplace was an obscure part of the world. It is one of those places that changed hands as the political climate changed. Lussdorf was part of the Austro-Hungarian Empire. Residents of this area considered themselves to be Bohemian.

She followed several of her children to the United States after her husband's death in 1895. She came to live with her daughter Theresia in Missouri. Grossmutter never learned to speak English. "If you wanted to talk to Grossmutter, you had to speak in German," according to my mother.

In the small Missouri town her church was the center of German life. The priest gave the sermon in German and she could confess her sins in German. The children in the household spoke to Grossmutter in German, or she ignored them.

The story of Grossmutter's leg has always fascinated me. It probably has acquired a life of its own. Apparently she had gangrene in one leg. The story I heard repeated was that "Grossmutter broke off her dead leg and threw it under the hospital bed."

No doubt that caused some consternation among the hospital staff. The story was reported in the local newspaper. Her family was not happy with this publicity. Her son Karl had a restaurant and having his customers read about his mother's antics in the hospital was bad for business.

I personally appreciate what must have been Grossmutter's reaction. Here was a lady in a hospital, probably for the first time in her life, at age ninety-three. She spoke no English. No wonder she was confused.

Grossmutter has been gone over seventy years. Her presence still lingers. A photo of her and her children hangs on my wall. All the women wear long black dresses; no one smiles. Her son Karl, the lone male, seems out of place with his mother and sisters. My grandson Stewart is fascinated by her and especially her name. He likes to say her name and cringe while he looks at the formidable group in the photo.

I like to claim her Bohemian roots for myself. Did she have a touch of gypsy in her? I use her as an example of a fortress in the storms of life. She survived moving to a new country, living in her daughter's home, and became a role model of independence I like to claim as my legacy.

Aunt Marie, AKA Rosie the Riveter

My Aunt Marie and Uncle Lloyd and their daughters Joann and Ruth lived in Missouri during the Depression years of the 1930s. Jobs were hard to find and Uncle Lloyd delivered milk for $1.00 a day. When he and his friend heard about better jobs in California, they left Missouri and went to find work. In 1938 Aunt Marie, my two cousins and Grandma Webster moved to California. Frank, the third child, was born there.

Aunt Marie joined the ranks of women known collectively as "Rosie the Riveter." She and the family were still in California when Japan attacked Pearl Harbor. Everyone had to do his or her part for the war effort. Both parents went to work at defense plants, at Lockheed and Northrop, making aircraft for the military. That's when Aunt Marie became one of the legendary Rosies. Before then she had done only office work and now she worked on an assembly line, manufacturing airplanes. She and my uncle had good paying jobs and they worked in defense plants until after the war ended.

The women who left the office or kitchen learned new skills. They had to dress for factory work, no frilly aprons and housedresses. The attire for an airplane factory was protective clothing. These included coveralls, hair pulled back or covered, safety glasses, safety shoes, and no jewelry.

Women became skilled at using riveting tools, welding torches, soldering irons and bundling multi-colored electrical wires into cables. Having male supervisors and coworkers introduced these women to the rough language of the workplace, a new experience for Aunt Marie. These guys called a spade a spade!

Aunt Marie and the other women made P-38 Lightning fighters on the assembly line. These planes are credited with the destruction of more Japanese aircraft than any other type of U.S. fighter.

For a while Grandma Webster lived with the family and cared for the children. When she returned to Missouri, Aunt Marie and Uncle Lloyd continued to work on separate shifts. They alternated on day and night shifts so someone was always home with the children. As my cousin Ruth told me, "We had to be quiet during the day as someone was *always* sleeping."

The family still tells the stories of rationing and shortages and blackouts at night. Lloyd was a block warden and helped patrol during the many blackouts. Many everyday items we take for granted were either rationed or unavailable. Hershey bars disappeared from grocery shelves. To get gas or tires for her car, Aunt Marie had to present a coupon. Sugar, coffee, and shoe purchases required a coupon besides the cash. It was a great time financially and the family prospered. They were eventually able to save enough money to buy a home after the war ended.

Aunt Marie's children are proud of the part their parents played to help win World War II. I am proud to have an aunt who was one of the women who put on coveralls and went to work, joining the war effort in factories across the nation.

Every year we honor the soldiers who landed at Normandy and fought and died there, and in all the battles of World War II. But at home, heroes like Rosie and the others made their successes possible. Rosie and all the folks on the home front deserve part of the glory. They too are part of "The Greatest Generation."

Aunt Cecilia's Honeymoon

I knew there *had* to be a story here. I sat at the table in my daughter Diane's kitchen one Thanksgiving afternoon, listening to the sound of conversations and reveling in the swirl of activity around me. Family of all degrees gathered in Dallas, and I planned to get stories from those I see only rarely.

Aunt Cecilia and her friend Florence reminisced about their early-married years. Both were war brides in 1943, in the midst of the World War II era.

Aunt Cecilia married my Dad's brother, Tom. Cecilia started telling me her story and I knew that this was the tale I came a thousand miles to hear. She began her story. "I met Tom at Fort Knox when he was in Army basic training there. He was a lonely soldier far from his Missouri home, and we got acquainted and started dating. We decided to get married in Louisville where my Mama and Daddy lived. None of Tom's family could come. They didn't have the money or the time to make the trip. What we decided to do was visit Tom's family on our honeymoon. We didn't have much money either, so Tom's brother in Missouri told us we could stay with them."

My Dad opened his home to the newlyweds. I say this rather loosely. My Dad, Mom and we, their three daughters, lived with my grandparents and two uncles in the family home. When the bride and

6

groom came to this house, they found nine other people in the four-bedroom house. A three-generation family shared those four bedrooms and one bathroom. My two sisters and I had one bedroom. We girls ranged in age from two to seven years.

"Tom and I slept in your room. You didn't seem to mind." Aunt Cecilia laughed at the memory. "We were in love and we had a free place to stay. Having a baby niece in our room didn't bother us!"

I spoke with my mother about this later. "I didn't let all of you stay in that room with them," Mom said. "I put you and Mary Ann on the couch downstairs." Mom obviously didn't want to be seen as letting three children interfere with the honeymooners. "Only two-year-old Helen was in the room in her baby bed. Uncle Tom and Aunt Cecilia slept in the double bed you and Mary Ann shared."

"So you and Uncle Tom had your honeymoon in our house with all of us, our grandparents and two uncles?" I asked. "That was a great start to a marriage."

"I guess so. We went on and had Dick and Lois and were married forty-five years until Tom died. It was a good beginning to a good life together."

"I had no idea that you as newlyweds were any different from any other guest we had in our house," I said. "What I do remember was your reading to me. You read me books about Penrod and Sam. You laughed so much when you read them I had no idea what they were about. Later I went to the library and got them for myself. I guess they were more interesting to you than they were to me."

Cecilia laughed again. "I do remember those books by Booth Tarkington. They were my favorite stories," she said. My memories of her will always be connected to those books, and her honeymoon spent in the bed I slept in.

Aunt Cecilia and Uncle Tom are both gone now. Her story is one of those similar to what Tom Brokaw put in his book *The Greatest Generation.* Most didn't get into Brokaw's book, but their stories are as important as those he told.

A family gathering is a rich source of history, stories, laughter and just plain fun. Go with a notebook, an open heart and open ears and you never know what you may come up with the next time you have writer's block!

My Family's Greatest Hero

I always knew that my cousin Jimmy Keane died on my ninth birthday, July 25, 1944. Years later I heard the story of Jimmy's death. As a result of being AWOL (Absent Without Leave), the brass in the Army gave Jimmy a choice -- be court-martialed or go on a European campaign. Since he chose the European campaign, he was in the June 6, 1944 Normandy invasion. He survived the brutal landing, but he died six weeks later of wounds.

I met Jimmy only once. He came to the front door of the Missouri home where my parents, sisters and I lived with my grandparents. He had come to visit his Grandma Hafner. When I saw him in uniform, I ran to my mother and said, "Uncle Sam is at the front door."

Of course it wasn't Uncle Sam. Jimmy had no business being there either. As it turned out, he was AWOL from the Army. Jimmy had a lifelong history of runaway escapades. His mother died when he was a child. He ran away from military school, from Father Flanagan's Boys' Town, and worst of all, from the U.S. Army.

By 1944 his father had died and his two younger sisters were orphans, living with relatives. Years later his sister Margaret received a letter from the Army asking her, as the oldest family member, if she wanted his remains to be returned to California, where she lived. Since Margaret had little income, she worried about the cost of relocation and burial. The government representative assured her there would be no charge if they buried him in a military cemetery. They did, and PFC James Francis Keane now lies in Golden Gate National Cemetery in San Bruno, California.

I met my cousin Jimmy only that one time. He is still in my memory as the personification of Uncle Sam and he is my family's greatest hero.

Memorial Day 1945

Memorial Day was always special. It was the last day of school. The day before was the day we went to the school picnic at Lake Contrary. I'd saved my allowance for a month so I could buy twelve tickets for the rides. They cost one dollar.

This year Mom didn't go because my sister Kathleen was just a two-month old baby. Mary Ann and Helen, my two younger sisters, and I went with Aunt Louise and our cousins Don, age eight and Dick, four. Aunt Louise drove Uncle Joe's big car, a La Salle. I liked not having to ride a bus to Lake Contrary.

Late in the afternoon we were all tired and dirty and most of our ride tickets were used up. I hated to leave the park and come home. Aunt Louise piled us in the car and drove home. On the way home I got to sit in front next to her because I was the oldest.

"Something's coming out of the car, Aunt Louise!" I saw flames coming out from under where the radio is. There was fire and smoke under my feet. I didn't think of anything except getting out of there.

"The car is on fire!" screamed Aunt Louise. She steered the car into the curb. It stopped suddenly and then turned over onto its side. I felt someone pull me out and say, "Stand here on the sidewalk. I'm getting the other kids out."

I watched as a man pulled out my sisters. A fire truck came and firemen dragged out the others. They put out the fire.

Aunt Louise started screaming, "My baby, my baby!" I was confused from all that was going on. Where was her baby? Who was her baby?

Dick was not with the children standing in the grass. I didn't quite understand what was going on. Was Dick in that fire? The firemen lifted the burning car from the grass. Dick was under the car. I was numb. Did that mean he will die?

A lady from the neighborhood came to take me and my sisters to her house. She called Mom and told her what happened. "Mrs. Webster," she said, "your children are all here with me. They are not hurt." I didn't know if she told Mom about Dick being under the burning car.

I heard an ambulance siren at the place where the car sat, still burning. The firemen were worried about it blowing up if they didn't get the fire out. Neighbors came and got all of us away from the car. Aunt Louise got in the ambulance with the doctors and nurses.

The lady drove us home to Mom. "I will be very careful to get you home. I know you must be afraid to get in a car."

Somehow I still had my purse. I saw that the few cents I had left were gone. This lady asked me how much money I lost. "About twenty-six cents," I told her. She got her purse and gave me fifty cents. She did the same thing for Mary Ann and Helen.

Home was less than a mile away. Mom was there caring for Kathleen. I don't remember this kind lady's name, but I do remember how she was so thoughtful to take care of us. She went home and Mom tried to help us understand how worried she was.

The next morning the *St. Joseph Gazette* had the story on the front page. Dick Hafner was the first fatality of the Memorial Day weekend. We went to the funeral home to be with the family. I wanted to look at him, but I was afraid of seeing him dead. He looked like he used to except he was dressed in a white suit. Dick would never wear a white suit and keep it clean!

Aunt Louise came up to us and hugged us. I wasn't sure why she did that. I guessed she was glad to see us and see we didn't get hurt. Later I realized we hadn't seen her since the wreck. After that she never drove a car again.

The funeral was the next day. Since Dick was only four years old, they didn't have a regular funeral Mass with black vestments. The priest wore white robes and said this is called the Mass of the Angels. Father Groetsch said that Dick is an angel in heaven. I hope so.

Every Memorial Day from then until now I remember that day and my cousin Dick.

Stephanie's Journey

My mother's cousin Stephanie was a woman of determination and grit, calling on every resource she could find. Her story is one of all those women who survive a war. Her spirit was like that of Scarlett O'Hara in *Gone With the Wind*. Scarlett came back to her home devastated by the American Civil War. Scarlett found her home and farm overrun with enemy invaders. The Union soldiers took everything from the home and the people in them. Scarlett had her field hands dig up yams from the ground. The only reason they didn't take the yams out of the ground was that those Yankees didn't know what they were. They thought they were just roots. This showed how completely a victorious army can ravage the conquered territory.

Stephanie's home was in the Sudetenland, a continent away from the rural Georgia of Scarlett in 1865. Stephanie survived World War II, first when it was overrun by the Nazis in 1939, and again when the Russians invaded the rural town of Lussdorf in 1945. Stephanie's family had lived in Lussdorf for 300 years. The Russian soldiers not only stole jewelry and valuables from the residents, they stole their homes and farms. As Stephanie said, "They took everything that could walk."

Men decide when and where to wage wars. Women come along

behind to rebuild what the men have torn down. They take on the job of rebuilding their lives and in the process salvage the family and civilization. Stephanie and Scarlett did this in two different countries in two different eras. This spirit of home-building and family is inherent in mothers in all times and cultures. Stephanie and Scarlett share a gutsy heritage that enabled them to face losing a war, their homes, friends and families. Both went on and built a new life for themselves and those who remained. Women pick up the pieces of their lives and go on. Like Scarlett, Stephanie used every strategy to get food, clothing and shelter for her family.

The war years made Stephanie a strong person. She faced running a farm and dairy operation with no man in the house. Her husband Gottfried was off fighting in faraway Norway. True, her father lived with her, but he was old and unable to do the heavy chores. Help came as prisoners of war. First Polish, then Russian prisoners were housed in Lussdorf. Stephanie took advantage of this forced labor to get her crops in. "In the six years that Gottfried was away I never missed a harvest," she told her friends. She saw to it that she shared what she had with the others in need, especially the older people whose sons were away at war.

Her daughter Ida and son Franz worked alongside their mother doing all the chores of a large farm. Ida plucked geese and used the feathers to make feather beds and down pillows. Franz tended the prizewinning dairy cattle. Lussdorf had a reputation for outstanding milk production. Its milk, rich in butterfat, was remarkable for the year 1944.

Cattle in this village were a valuable asset. That is why having the enemy take "everything that could walk" was so devastating. As

World War II was ending in May 1945, Russian troops arrived on horseback and took away everything of value. All rooms were searched for valuables. The suffering of the girls and women began. Fifteen-year-olds, even seventy-year-old women were not spared. Several villagers chose to end their own lives.

Czech partisans and Russians took over the houses of the German-speaking population and expelled them from their homes. People were driven home from the fields and had to gather within twenty minutes in front of the schoolhouse.

In 1946, it looked as if she and her family would become homeless. The Czech population long regarded their German-speaking neighbors with suspicion. When the invading Russians started rounding up local citizens, some villagers chose to become collaborators with the enemy. In this way they hoped to gain some favor and be spared death. What the Czech collaborators did to the German-speaking villagers was make sure that they were expelled.

Stephanie's home had been in the Fiedler family for 300 years. Even Scarlett couldn't claim such a long history at Tara. Scarlett regained Tara. Stephanie lost her home and the family history it represented. Gottfried arrived home in 1946 to see the devastation of his family and home. When he registered with the town officials, they told him, "You may stay in your home if you have a job."

Naturally, Gottfried said, "I am a carpenter. I can help rebuild."

The blunt answer was, "There are no jobs." Here was a soldier returning from fighting a war back to his own home. The problem was that now it was not his homeland anymore. "You and your family must leave Lussdorf," said an official.

Stephanie, Gottfried, and their two children began the trek west.

The displaced population grew larger by the day as they walked westward away from the Russians. Every town they passed through was the same, full of hungry homeless refugees. Local people had barely enough food for themselves, much less for thousands of strangers.

With her house in the hands of strangers, her husband without a job, and the family now on its way to Germany, Stephanie made up her mind. "We will not give up. We will find help any way we can." When the family arrived in Germany they found conditions were what one could expect after a war had just ended.

Housing was the immediate problem. Those homes left standing were partially bombed-out and dangerous. Every day Stephanie was out early looking for better shelter for the family. She found an unoccupied house that still stood. That was about all one could say about it. It was drafty and cold. "I brought as much warm clothing as I could carry, but still Ida and Franz are cold." At age fourteen and seven, the children outgrew coats and shoes in a short time.

"Surely if my aunt knew how desperate we are, she would help us. Living in America for all these years, she must be rich." There was a problem. Letters she had sent during the war came back. "Maybe she is dead or has moved."

"How can I let my American relatives know how bad the living conditions here are?" She pondered this question relentlessly. She had sent letters when no mail was allowed out of Germany. The letters came back, and she searched for another way to contact them. Then she remembered her childhood neighbor, Sophie, who moved to America before the war.

She wrote to Sophie for help on January 10, 1947. "I was forced to leave my dear homeland and Germany will have to be our new homeland. For your parents, dear Sophie, I have done lots of nice things, when during winter they were without milk products. Please be so nice and write a few lines to my aunt in English so that I may know if she is still alive. My husband came home eight days before we had to leave."

Sophie wrote to Stephanie's aunt and cousin in America on March 23, 1947. "I am writing to you at the request of your niece, Stephanie, your brother's daughter who once was my neighbor in Lussdorf. You probably have heard or read about the removal of all German peoples out of the Sudetenland and how these people are now scattered throughout Germany as refugees.

"Your niece has a family and with her mother is now living in Germany.

"She has tried several times to contact you and for some reason or other has failed to receive a reply from you. I believe that is why she has written to me and asked if I might try to get in touch with you. Here's hoping that Stephanie will hear from you soon."

Reading Sophie's letter and hearing the desperation in Stephanie's letter, her Aunt Theresia and Cousin Margaret wrote back to Stephanie, "We have a letter from your friend Sophie. Our letters to you in Lussdorf have been returned. We thought you must have been killed in the war. We want to help you. Send us a list of what you need. Send sizes of clothing for yourselves and your children."

Margaret and Theresia sent basic food items to Stephanie. "Once we have clothing sizes, we can send the right things for them." Margaret wrote a letter first, and then mailed the package of food to the address in Germany, Stephanie's new home.

The timing was just right. Stephanie received the letter early in December 1947. Later a package arrived. Stephanie's immense joy came through in the letter she wrote to her cousin Margaret, "The letter arrived one week ago, the package on Christmas evening. We had a great surprise because I had no other presents for us. There is nothing for money. My boy was in a hurry to open the package. Because he wanted to see his shoes. They fit him very well and he went to church with them on Christmas. The stockings and socks are very fine. Dear Margaret, the coat fits well to me and my daughter, it is very nice. Please send me the black overcoat and still the other you have written. Ida has only one coat and it is too small."

What Stephanie didn't realize was that she had tapped into a network of strong women in America. Margaret told her sister Mathilda of the desperation in Stephanie's letters. A box arrived from cousin Mathilda with clothing and other needed items. Stephanie decided to get more specific about what she needed. Her next letter included the following excerpts: "In unpacking the box I could not weep but tears of joy, for I got the nice feeling that we are not alone and not forsaken. Once more many thanks for the exceeding love.

"Nowadays this kind of cooking is new to me. At home we were never at a loss for anything. Dear Mathilda, I'll write some things which we can't buy over here. The most important things will be underlined.

1. dried whole milk
2. shortening
3. cocoa
4. whole egg powder."

Again Stephanie showed her spirit of determination to get help.

Not only did she ask for what she needed, she was specific about priorities.

Conditions did not improve much by March 1950. Stephanie wrote to cousin Mathilda, "Since I had written you the last time here is much changed. In June 1948 we got new money. Now all the shops have enough food and clothes. But we have no money to go shopping.

"Since the twelfth of April (1949) we have a little boy named Erich. He is soon one year old. We all love him very much.

"We think every day on our dear home. There we had all, and here we are so very poor. We have such bad room, wet and cold. And we have not enough furniture. We need all our money to buy food."

The cousins responded so that baby Erich would not be left out at Christmas. They sent baby clothes and toys for a little boy.

In 1951, Stephanie wrote, "Many thanks for your package. It was indeed a surprise to receive it on New Year, and we were very happy. Little Erich was glad about those cars especially, he also liked the chocolate you sent. The clothings [sic] for him fit very well, and he looks really good in the red pants. He is such a nice little fellow and everybody in the house seems to like him."

Christmas 1951, another package arrived. A delighted Stephanie wrote to Margaret. "Your dear letter and package I've got, many thanks to you. Erich took the toy, the bear, with himself into his bed, and he was not able to sleep during half the night, and all with joy. This time we celebrated Christmas for the sixth time in a foreign country, but we hope and wish, that we once may come back to our native country . . .

"Since the month July we have changed our dwelling place, and now we live in a small town. In our town there are no American soldiers but they are garrisoned in the nearest town. Have you any acquaintances who are as soldiers here in Germany? If yes, please write them our address that they can pay us a visit. It would be all right and fine, if we in Germany had not so many men out of work; the cause is the high population. Here is a great many of homeless people and they all must live here."

An American soldier brought another source of help. A family friend, Dick, was stationed in Germany as part of the American occupation forces. He visited Stephanie's family, bringing candy and cigarettes and a feeling of friendship from America that remains today.

No more letters came until 1966. Stephanie's husband, Gottfried, wrote to Margaret, "Much has changed during the time we didn't write one another. Your cousin, Stephanie, my wife, has died on April 12, 1957, after a difficult operation in the hospital."

Stephanie survived a war and years of poverty and deprivation in a new country. She was never able to return to her homeland. Today her children live in Germany and have prospered. In 1989, after the fall of Communism, Stephanie's daughter Ida went back to visit the family home in Lussdorf.

"It was a sad trip. I looked at my mother's home that had been in the family for 300 years and wept. Strangers who are Czech live there now. They think it is really their home. I came away with a sadness that still exists. I also came away with a feeling that I will never go back. That part of my life has ended and now I will go on with the rest of my life. My mother would not understand this and I am glad she did not have to see her home in the hands of strangers."

Stephanie survived a war and found a way to keep her family

together in spite of losing her home and even her native homeland. She found a way to get on with life in a new country and managed to keep her family fed and alive. Perhaps the greatest tribute to her hope for the future lays in the person of Erich, a baby born in a new land and welcomed with such great joy as expressed in her own words. She is truly a woman for all times.

Remembering the Dinner Party

When I helped Mom clean out the house she had lived in for eighty-seven years, I found the ricer that she used to make applesauce. A ricer is a cone-shaped aluminum device with holes in it, set on a wooden frame. You cook quartered apples and squish them through the holes with a wooden paddle. The seeds and peels stay inside and only applesauce comes out. It was the last piece of a set of WearEver pots and pans that Mom and Dad bought years before.

Seeing it took me back to that summer evening sixty years ago when she and Dad had their dinner party. My parents weren't party people. If we had people over for dinner, they were family. This was different.

Mr. Weaver was a salesman whose job was to impress prospective buyers with his WearEver line of pans. His sales pitch was, "I'll cook a meal for you and your guests and show you how good the pans cook and how easy they are to clean up."

Mom said, "You children eat early so Mr. Weaver can fix dinner in peace. I'll fix fried chicken, your favorite meal." I knew what Mom was up to. She wanted us to stay out of the way during the big dinner party. Mary Ann and Helen, my younger sisters and I weren't too happy eating in the kitchen when we knew the guests would dine later in the dining room. After we ate, Mom shooed us outside. "Stay in the yard and play," she said. Mr. Weaver came into the house with pots, pans and bags of food.

Helen started crying when she heard pots and pans clattering inside the house. "I'm still hungry and I know they are having something good that we didn't get," she said.

"We already ate, so quit crying," I said. Mary Ann started to cry and I felt like crying too.

Helen wandered next door where our favorite neighbors, Mr. and Mrs. Eytcheson were picking tomatoes in their garden.

"Why are you crying, all three of you?" asked Mr. Eytcheson.

"Mom and Dad are having dinner and won't let us come in to eat," Helen said. Mary Ann and I gasped and looked at each other.

"I'll bet your folks don't know how hungry you are. I'll go ask them if they forgot you," he said.

"No, don't do that. They have company and someone is cooking dinner for them. He wants them to buy some pans," I said. I couldn't let the neighbors think my parents didn't feed us. I would get Helen for doing this.

"Well, we'll just see what we can find inside for you," said Mrs. Eytcheson. She went inside and brought out lemonade and a plate of cookies.

Mr. Eytcheson said, "I saw Mr. Weaver's car. You can stay here till the dinner is over." The neighbors were familiar with Mr. Weaver's car. They had bought a set of pans too. Mrs. Eytcheson gave us more lemonade and we sat on their porch till Dad came over to get us.

"Why are you over here? Didn't Mom tell you to stay in our

yard?" Dad asked.

I was holding my breath. Helen blurted out, "Mrs. Eytcheson gave us cookies and lemonade because we were hungry. You didn't let us eat with you." I knew we were in for it.

"Come home *now*," said Dad. Mom and Dad weren't parents who spanked children, but we knew very well that what we did was not acceptable.

"For your punishment you will do the dishes from our dinner," said Dad. The kitchen was full of dirty dishes. Mr. Weaver was in the middle of the mess. I think he used every pan in the set. He cooked a roast, made applesauce with the ricer and used every size pan he could find to cook vegetables.

But he was a nice man and helped us clean up. Part of the sales pitch was to show Mom how easy it was to clean up his cookware. We finished in the kitchen and were sent to bed. The next day Mom cleared out her cabinets to hold all the new pots and pans. They were new, shiny and heavy, and I enjoyed learning to cook with Mom's new toys.

My favorite piece was that ricer. No one else's mother had such a tool. They bought applesauce in a can or made it with lots more work, peeling apples and cutting them up in small pieces and mashing them with a potato masher.

As I helped Mom clean out the old home place, she said, "I won't have room for all this stuff in a small apartment like I'm going to. Do you want anything from my kitchen?"

I spoke up right away. Most of the WearEver set was gone or not usable anymore. But not the ricer. "I'd really like that ricer you used to make applesauce. I haven't made any for years because it was more trouble than it was worth."

"It's yours," Mom said. "I don't use it anymore and I know you'd use it."

Now sixty years later the Eytchesons are gone, Mom lives in a retirement apartment and I have that ricer in my cabinet. When I use it, I go back in time to that summer evening when Mom and Dad had their dinner party and my sisters and I weren't invited. As I think about it now, I have a different feeling about not being included in that gathering. I can laugh at how my sisters and I reacted. I get a warm feeling about my parents and their one dinner party that I didn't attend.

Cherries and Arthritis

The headline in the local newspaper read: "Arthritis Pain Sufferers in Jubilee about Tart Cherries." It goes on to relate stories about a Michigan man who bought a half gallon of cherry concentrate to help relieve the swelling and pain in his hands and knuckles. After taking this stuff for two months, his pain was gone.

I am on intimate terms with arthritis, rheumatoid arthritis, to be precise. I know RA from over thirty years of joint pain, medications that helped, medications that did nothing, medications that caused kidney, heart and skin problems. I have had surgery on both hands and both feet to alleviate the results of this disease. I survive and I thrive.

I've tried raisins soaked in gin, copper bracelets and a North Carolina Indian healer named Chief Two Trees. I've rejected many other bizarre "cures," such as bee stings, to make RA better. I haven't given up, but it does get tedious sometimes.

But now cherries appear on the scene. I know cherries better than I know arthritis. I grew up with two tart cherry trees in my very own back yard. When I was born, my parents planted a cherry tree in my honor. When my sister Mary Ann was born a year later, she also got a cherry tree. I must say that I'm glad my parents quit planting trees with the birth of my two younger sisters, Helen and Kathleen. That would have made *four* cherry trees in the Webster back yard.

As we girls grew, so did those cherry trees. I learned to hate ripe cherry season about Decoration Day, as the Memorial holiday is called in Missouri. Once the cherries got ripe, Mary Ann and I had our jobs. One picked cherries; the other pitted cherries. I don't know which is worse. Occasionally Dad picked and Mary Ann and I pitted. And pitted. It seems like every day there were gallons and gallons more cherries.

One especially irritating aspect was that school had just ended on Decoration Day. Did we get to have a vacation or a week at the beach? No way! Cherries were on our agenda the first few weeks of summer vacation. I couldn't even go to the library until those damn cherry trees were bare!

We had a typical 1940s home, no air conditioning. That added more misery to taking seeds out of cherries. My arms dripped with cherry juice and my face dripped with sweat. This definitely was piecework, with not much variety. I got so bored with it that finding a worm inside the cherry was the high point of the day. "Look, I found a worm. Can I throw this one out?"

Of course the answer was "Yes." The bummer part was that I'd already done the pitting. If I could only tell the wormy ones *before* I pulled out the seed, I'd save that one job.

Mom canned the fruit and made pies and jam from the cherries. She called them "pie cherries." I called them sour cherries. I would have worked with more gusto if they had been the dark sweet Bing cherries I saw at the grocery store. But, no, that kind didn't grow in our yard. These pie cherries were very small and a gallon must have contained 5000 pieces. About the time my bowl was empty, Dad would come in with another full bucket. "Here's some more!"

"Isn't it about time for lunch?" Mary Ann and I were ready to quit, but the best we could hope for was a lunch break. Lunch was haphazard with bowls of cherries all over the kitchen counters, canning jars standing ready to be filled, and the canning pot boiling up. After lunch, in the heat of the afternoon, Mom would load quart jars of cherries into that cauldron and process the fruit. By evening we had rows of jars sealed and ready to store in the basement for winter use.

The worst part was realizing that the tree was still loaded with more cherries and tomorrow would be a repeat of today. If it looked like rain, Dad would pick late into the evening so we'd have work even if it rained.

Years later, after I was married I would go pick cherries for my own family. Mom encouraged us to "Come help me get rid of those cherries so I don't have to do it alone." Mary Ann did that years after I moved away and left Missouri. One year I came home to see Mom canning cherries with the seeds in them. "Why?" I asked.

"No one would help me, so I just put them up with seeds in them." I guess when we ate a pie filled with both seeds and cherries, we got the point. The trees are gone now and none are in their place. The home that had been in Mom's family for 100 years is no longer her home. Mom lives in a senior high rise in Kansas City.

Cherries from Michigan are one of the latest fads to relieve the pain of arthritis. I have another take on those cherries. I think maybe taking seeds out of those millions of cherries may be the reason I have rheumatoid arthritis today. I must have worn out my finger joints before I got out of high school with those dreaded cherry-pitting days of early summer. I am not about to put a cherry concentrate into my body.

Mary Ann and Me

For fourteen months I was an only child, the alpha female. Then a kid sister came into my life. She was born on September 8, the same day as our Grandfather Hafner's birthday. That gave her status that I didn't enjoy. Even her name was special, Mary Ann, so named because September 8 is also the feast of the birth of the Blessed Virgin Mary! I guess I did adjust to the newcomer. Old faded black-and-white photos show us playing together, sharing a birthday cake in the yard, and romping in the snow in the winter and with the garden hose in the summer.

We spent summers at home, swimming in the local pool, walking to the library. And helping with the two younger sisters who joined the family. Helen and Kathleen were the "babies" we didn't include in our games. Our other summer chores included canning the cherries, tomatoes, beans, and peaches from our garden.

By August the days were getting long, hot and boring. We had exhausted all the good books at the library. The municipal pool was getting too crowded to be fun, and we were tired of helping can the fruits and vegetables from the garden.

We started going down the street to see Mrs. McNamara. She had two nieces who came for a week's visit every August. She and Mr. McNamara had no children and she had asked Mom "Would you let

Pat and Mary Ann come and play with Barbara and Nadine?" That solved two problems, what to do with her guests and filling our boring days.

Mom didn't hesitate. "Sure, they can walk down whenever you want them." This was a couple weeks before the girls would arrive.

I'm sure we made pests of ourselves going down to her house and asking, "When will Barbara and Nadine be here?" They lived on a farm in King City, about twenty-five miles from St. Joe, our home.

We finally got the word, "They'll be here next Sunday evening. Their Dad will bring them after Sunday dinner. He'll pick them up the next Saturday. You can come about nine o'clock Monday morning."

I still remember those special days. For a lady who had no children Mrs. McNamara knew how to please these four children. None of our parents gave us the fun activities she did.

Lunch was like nothing we had at home, no bologna sandwiches and canned tomato soup and milk. We had chicken salad sandwiches and potato chips, and Pepsi to drink. Later in the afternoon she served ice cream and cake, just like a birthday party. But it was no one's birthday. This was a treat for all of us.

Some afternoons we played card games, like Old Maid, Crazy Eights and Rummy. The highlight of the day was Bingo. She gave us Bingo cards and real counters to cover the numbers. Best of all there were real prizes for the winners. It might be a quarter or a small toy, but it was a prize.

The adults allowed us to take the bus downtown and show off our big city to these farm girls. We had a little money to spend and made Woolworth's five-and ten-cent store one of our stops. Mary Ann and I were dedicated customers of this place. Mostly we walked around and visited the Pony Express memorial. St. Joe was proud of this historical site. We took the elevator to the thirteenth floor of the Corby Building, the tallest one in town.

Too soon the week ended and our new friends left for home. We promised to write each other and be together next August. A few weeks later school began and we were back into the fall and winter routines.

But next summer was coming soon, and we looked forward to seeing Barbara and Nadine. Years later I think back on these lazy summer days with a sense of how simple life was then. I appreciate the good days Mary Ann and I had with Mrs. McNamara and her nieces. We grew up, married, and had families. When we gather for family reunions we think back on these simple summer days.

Grandma Webster's Chocolate Chip Cookies

"Watch where you bite, these are Grandma Webster's cookies," said my mother. My sisters and I loved those BIG cookies, but we had to be careful eating them. Grandma Webster made the biggest chocolate chip cookies in the world. Mom did make cookies, but rather small ones. Grandma's saucer-sized cookies had one problem that Mom's didn't. Her cookies had booby traps in them, black walnut shells.

Grandma Webster was my Dad's mother, a widow who lived in a tiny apartment above the Jerre Anne Cafeteria. She worked for Jerre Anne's, making pies, cooking chicken and preparing fresh vegetables. Even after she retired, she'd go down every day to "snap beans." We all knew she went to be with people and to get the local gossip.

The cookie nut of choice in my area of Northwestern Missouri was the black walnut. Dad, my sisters, and I would go out in October and pick up the walnuts. Preparing black walnuts for cookies is a long process. Pick up the nuts, still in their green covering. Spread them out on the ground to dry the hulls till they are black. Keep squirrels at bay so they won't steal these nuts. Pound off the outer hulls. This was the easy part. These nuts have rigid shells, unlike pecans or peanuts. Dad pounded them apart with a hammer. Now the nuts were ready for taking out the meat. We used needles, nails, nutpicks, whatever we could find, to pick out the meat. After we prepared walnuts, we always had black hands from the juice. In all those years of nut picking, we never thought to use rubber gloves to protect our hands. It became the trademark of our labors.

Grandma's eyes were those of a seventy-year-old and she did not see all the tiny shell fragments in her cookie dough. We learned to be careful when we bit down on these cookies. We were ready to hit a piece of shell. No one ever broke a tooth, but no one ever mentioned these barriers to Grandma.

Did Grandma ever realize that we ate cookies with nutshells in them? No. Grandma never ate any of her cookies. When I asked Mom why not, she told me. "Your Grandma has diabetes and can't eat food with sugar in it."

That was an awesome thought to me. Here was a woman doing all this work of preparing food she could not eat. She cooked pies, cookies and cakes and never ate them.

Homemade cookies were but a part of Grandma's legacy to me. She taught me about doing things for those you love just because you love them. She taught me that diabetes wouldn't stop her life and devotion to her family. Years later as I now struggle with arthritis, I think of Grandma Webster's cookies and how she made them for us and never ate any.

When my granddaughter Amy visits me, we make chocolate chip cookies. The difference is that we use a mix from a box with nuts already prepared inside. I tell Amy about her great-grandma Webster and the nutshells I ate as a child. We laugh together, take the cookies out of the oven. "I like them best when they're hot and we drink a glass of milk with them," says Amy. I'm carrying on my grandmother's legacy and someday maybe Amy will make cookies with another generation.

Whatever Happened to Baby Chick?

What my sister Kathleen learned at the family reunion was not a pleasant story. Twenty Websters gathered at Edisto Island, South Carolina for the Easter holiday. Our ninety-year-old mother came along. So did assorted cousins and nieces and nephews.

The conversation came around to reminiscing about Easters past. "Do you remember when we got colored baby chicks at Easter?" asked Kathleen. In those days, the 1950s, buying colored chicks was one of the rites of Easter.

"Sure," I said. "I got one every year, so did you. We used to watch how the feathers changed. The colored feathers gradually grew out and the chicken got white feathers. They got bigger and started flying and running away. We had to keep chasing them back into our yard, so the neighbor's dog wouldn't get them."

"When he started crowing at dawn," Mom said, "the neighbors complained that he was just a pest. But you insisted on keeping that rooster."

"I loved my little green chick. I called him Baby. He would follow me around. I tried to get Mom to let him sleep in my room. I wonder what ever happened to those chickens. I don't remember them growing up and flying away," said Kathleen.

"You don't remember what we did with those chickens?" asked Mom. "Dad wrung their necks and we cooked them! We had them for dinner."

"No, I didn't eat my baby chicken!" said Kathleen. "You're teasing me, like you always did when I was little."

Mom was extremely blunt, as always. "Yes, Dad would wring their necks and we cleaned them and cooked them. I guess you never made the connection."

"I can't believe you really did that! Pat, did you know we ATE our pet chickens?" Kathleen was horrified at what she had just heard.

"Sure, I knew. I watched Dad kill them. I guess they did it when you were taking a nap," I said. "Mom put the dead chicken in boiling water, pulled off all the feathers, cleaned out the guts and cut it up to cook."

To this day Kathleen finds it hard to look at a whole fryer in the grocery store without a twinge of pain remembering how she found out about the fate of her pet Easter chick. She's glad no one sells green baby chicks anymore for Easter baskets.

What My Father Taught Me

I always think of my Dad, Beauford Webster, when Derby Day rolls around. As far as I know Dad never attended a Kentucky Derby. I doubt if he ever bet on a horse in the race. He was not that kind of guy.

What he did was visit his brother Tom in Louisville. Uncle Tom was stationed at Fort Campbell, Kentucky during World War II. He married a local young lady, Cecilia. After World War II, he and Aunt Cecilia stayed in Louisville.

For most of my childhood, my family did not take vacations. There was no money to spend on trips or travel. One year, however, Mom and Dad did take a trip to see Uncle Tom and his bride in Louisville. We children were not invited. I remember the feeling I had as I saw Mom and Dad board the train at Union Station. I was angry and jealous. How could they go away and leave us with Grandma? We lived in the same house with Grandma, so she was no stranger, but I resented not being invited on such a trip.

While in Louisville, Dad and Mom toured Churchill Downs and Calumet Farm, the ultimate tourist spot in Kentucky. When Dad got home, he was a fan of the Derby for the rest of his life. He followed the stories of the race; he listened to it on the radio. He spoke of Calumet Farm in hushed tones, describing the silo on the grounds as being an exact replica of the Calumet baking powder can. Calumet baking powder was a staple in my mother's kitchen, so seeing it every time we baked reinforced my memory of it. The can has the unique colors of Calumet Farm's jockeys' uniform, devil's red and blue racing colors. The Indian in full headdress is the trademark still seen today on the baking powder can.

Dad hooked me into Derby Day too. I listened to it with him. Whirlaway and Citation and jockey Eddie Arcaro are names I remember best. Today Calumet Farm has lost its past glory and reputation; it no longer exists as it was when Dad saw it. Dad didn't live long enough to experience the collapse of the famous farm's empire.

Dad passed away in 1961. I was married and gone from Missouri where I grew up. Hearing the hype for Derby Day each May is another special memory of Dad.

Just as my Dad never saw a Kentucky Derby race, he never saw a World Series baseball game in person. The family budget didn't include baseball games. Once there was a TV in the house, however, he arranged to watch World Series games. The Missouri team was the St. Louis Cardinals. Dad didn't care which teams played.

In the 1950s, Series games were not necessarily in the evening hours as they now are. Most fields didn't have lights, so the games were played during the afternoon. Having a job at the local meat packing plant prevented Dad from watching the afternoon games. Once he got enough seniority to have first choice, Dad asked for one week's vacation the first week of October. I remember coming home from school and hearing the game on television.

"Do you take your vacation just to watch television?" I asked.

"That seems sort of silly."

"You know we never go anywhere, so what I do is take this week to watch a couple World Series games. Your mother manages to find something for me to do in the morning. Tomorrow I'm supposed to paint the kitchen and I think I'm scheduled to clean out the basement the next day."

To a young person today, this may seem like an extremely boring way to spend a vacation. I grew up in a time still reeling from the Great Depression. St. Joseph, Missouri did not prosper as much as other places as a result of World War II. But Derby Day and the World Series were Dad's favorite vacation spots, right in the living room.

My Dad did teach me life lessons though I don't think he ever realized it. I didn't fully understand his lessons until many years later. What he taught me haunts me daily as I struggle with the effects of rheumatoid arthritis. Dad suffered with RA in the 1960s when aspirin and cortisone were the only medications available. He died at age fifty-three of kidney complications that I am sure were compounded by the cortisone. His doctor did no testing to monitor this powerful medication. When he finally knew something was wrong, Dad's kidney function was poor. He was hospitalized and died a few weeks later.

Dad was the paymaster who handed checks to 1500 employees every Friday. A meat packing plant is not a user-friendly place for anyone, man or animals, especially a man with RA. The floors are brick or concrete, hard and often very slippery. The temperature for processing meat mandated by Federal inspectors is 36-45 degrees. The freezer for storing the meat is colder yet. Dad walked many miles every Friday through the coolers, freezers, and heated offices to give folks paychecks. He was a popular man. One coworker told me at his funeral: "Everyone likes to see Beauford coming."

I can still hear his footsteps in the morning as he came down the stairs in our home. I did not realize at the time just how difficult that was for him. I too struggle as I walk down stairs. I now remember how his footfalls sounded and I am sure mine sound like that. He rose early, making his instant coffee and toast before anyone else was up. I often got up as early and still do. Perhaps I learned from his behavior that early rising is possible even with arthritis. We had no car; he either rode two buses or had a ride from a friend. His workday started at 7:00 A.M.

Dad's lessons to me were that one does not stay home from work because his feet hurt, or it is hard to walk. I think how hard it must have been to walk up and down those metal stairs, often slick with pork fat, in and out of the freezers, coolers and into the steamy room where scalding water removed hair from pigs floating in a tank. His hands most likely felt the effects of the extremes of cold and heat. Yet I never heard him complain about his disease.

His devotion to his faith rubbed off on me too. We were a Catholic family and there was no way I could talk them into letting me go to Central High School, two blocks from home. No, I went to the Convent of the Sacred Heart, the Catholic girl's school. The Catholic boys went to Christian Brothers High School, several miles away. We Convent girls wore uniforms, curtsied to the nuns and had rigid rules about behavior and keeping our virginity. I did it all.

Dad had a devotion to his faith and the faith life of his church that remains with me today. He was the head usher who recruited and assigned ushers for four Sunday Masses each week. He attended most of the old traditional services in the Catholic Church of the 1950s. Today many of these are gone. I must admit I don't miss most of them. But I do have a deeply imbedded regard for my faith life. It has been amended somewhat, but I feel Dad gave me that solid beginning.

I was married and living away from my hometown when Dad died. I had a new baby and four other preschoolers. I went to see him on the train from Omaha. I had not been on a train for years. I had recently seen the Lincoln funeral car on display in a railroad museum in Omaha, where we lived. I had the feeling I was on that same train. The seats were scratchy mohair and of a vintage that must have been Civil War era.

Dad was not aware of my coming. He was incoherent and unresponsive. That is, until his brother Tom arrived from Kentucky. Dad recognized Uncle Tom and started talking to him. His words were, "Tom help me!" Of course Tom had no way to help and it upset him and my Grandmother Webster who was in the room at the time.

Dad died a few days later. His friends came in large numbers both nights of the funeral home visitations. He had several gatherings of friends and colleagues. The funeral was a Catholic Mass at Immaculate Conception Church, where Dad had been the head usher. I am told that the funeral rituals are for the living, and I do agree with that. My sisters and I went home with Mom to her large house to help her cope. She lived on in that house for thirty-five more years. For several years when I came to visit with my large family, I expected to hear Dad's unique footsteps coming down the stairs.

Kelly's Special Delivery

My cousin Ruth's story of her daughter's special delivery is one of our family's unique stories. I recorded this story from Ruth in her own words. PWS

"How will I know I'm in labor?" I asked my friends.

"Oh, don't worry, you'll know," they said.

This was 1964, pre-pill, pre-information highway, the dark ages. Since most of my friends were single, they had no birthing experience to help me out. The few married women I knew repeated the mantra, "You'll know . . ." usually followed by a story of their own to support their theory.

I was living in Bad Tölz, Germany where my husband Stony was a civilian employee working with the military. Bad Tölz was a beautiful town nestled in the Bavarian Alps, about thirty miles south of Munich. We were eligible for all military privileges, including medical care, which was excellent. But I would have to go to Munich to deliver my baby in the hospital. I felt that I needed a little more information than I was receiving. I wrote to a friend in the states asking her to help me out. She promptly sent me a copy of *Childbirth Without Fear, The Principles and Practice of Natural Childbirth* by Grantly Dick Read. I read it from cover to cover. I was ready! Bring it on!

This was the Alps, and by October 19, we had plenty of snow. My baby was due any day now. I woke feeling fine, a little backache, but nothing to worry about. I busied myself cleaning and checking the new baby's room to be sure that everything was ready. I was sure he would arrive soon.

Around 3 P.M. the backache was worse, so I decided to drive myself to the dispensary to let a doctor check me out. The doctor checked me briefly. "You must get to the hospital *now*," he said.

"I want to call my husband at work so he can drive me to the hospital," I said.

"You don't have time to call your husband. I'm calling an ambulance," said the doctor.

I did prevail and called Stony who worked nearby and asked him to bring me a nightgown when he came to the hospital. I had not prepared for an overnight stay.

The ambulance arrived a few minutes later. I was in the back on a cot. Before we took off, Stony arrived with a nightgown he had picked up at the PX on his way over. He would follow the ambulance in his car. In the ambulance he kissed me good-bye.

Before Stony could get out, the ambulance door slammed shut, and we were on our way. In this ambulance were Mike, a Specialist 4 (Sp4,) a driver, my husband and me, in labor.

Before long the driver noticed the gas gauge. "We're going to have to stop for gas if we are going to make it to Munich," he said. "I have to get gas on the *kaserne* (army base), so we have to make a slight detour. Are you OK back there?"

"So far, so good," I said. We got the gas and started out on the Autobahn. I tried to recall the words of wisdom from my book. The backache was much worse. In fact the ache had turned into real pains. "Yes, this must be labor. I must be in the first stage. What to do? Oh, yes. Breathe. What else?" I couldn't remember.

"Stony, what do I do now?" I asked.

"I haven't read the book, honey. How about breathing?" he asked.

He was no help. Now I was in real pain. I started screaming. The Sp4 climbed into the back of the ambulance. The driver drove like one is allowed to do on the German Autobahn. There are no speed limits. Stony tried to comfort me. "The baby is coming out *NOW*!" I screamed.

"Don't worry, Mrs. Schaefle, you'll know." The words of my friends came back to me. I knew now they weren't just whistling Dixie.

We finally arrived on the outskirts of Munich. "The hospital is right across the railroad tracks. I can see it," said Stony.

Both he and the Sp4 told me, "Push. Push, Mrs. Schaefle."

That part was easy. The baby arrived. "Thank God, I'm done," I said.

"No, no not yet," the Sp4 said. "The baby is feet first and you still have to deliver the head." It was a breech birth. "Push, push," he said again.

I did and the baby arrived just as the train arrived. We all sat at the railroad crossing with the new baby while the train crossed. I was pooped. I didn't care what else was going on.

Stony was ecstatic. "It's a boy. We'll name him Kelly after my boss and good friend," he said.

"Sounds good to me," I said. Stony put Kelly on my stomach, cord intact, and we finally got to the hospital.

Later my husband told me that my vocabulary during this time left a little to be desired. Even an army driver and the Sp4 were shocked. I couldn't really remember.

When we arrived at the hospital, my husband rushed inside yelling, "Help, help, my wife just had a baby boy on the Autobahn. Here's her records."

"Calm down, Sgt. Schaeffer, your wife couldn't have just had a baby. She's only six weeks pregnant," said a nurse after she read the papers he handed her. They had obviously given us the records for Schaeffer, not Schaefle.

Meanwhile, the doctors examined my baby as I was lying in the hallway on a cot, smoking a cigarette. (Yes, I know. But this was 1964 and we all smoked. Who knew?) I felt great. There is something to be said for natural childbirth.

After a long examination, the doctor came in and said, "Mr. and Mrs. Schaefle, your baby girl is fine. We want to keep her downstairs in the nursery for a few days."

"Girl?" Yes, her. My husband had made a mistake. "It was an honest mistake," he said. "It was dark in that ambulance and when I saw the cord, I thought it was a boy."

It was his first delivery and what could one expect. "Let's keep the name Kelly for her," I said. We both liked it and at the time it was unique. She was, and always has been, a beautiful healthy girl, none the worse for her mother's stupidity.

The hospital considered me contaminated since I had given birth outside the hospital. That meant I was not on the obstetrical floor. I could not visit outside my room. Only staff and my husband could visit me. Even baby Kelly was not allowed in my room until I was ready to go home.

This was a time long before the days of camcorders in the delivery room, where everyone is welcome. Now whole families participate in childbirth. This is not a criticism of the system of that era. I am pointing out how much things have changed.

I am eternally grateful to the driver of that ambulance who performed above and beyond his call of duty and I give credit to Mike, that Sp4 who helped Stony and me deliver a healthy baby, breech at that. I will always appreciate the excellent medical treatment my family and I received from military and civilian personnel.

My second daughter, Joanna, was born in that same hospital four years later. Yes, in the *hospital*. Believe me, I was there in plenty of time. I knew this time around when I was actually in labor. I didn't have to ask anybody.

The Sound of Silence

Expectant mothers: What sounds does your developing child hear and feel while he or she is inside your uterus? I wondered about that through seven pregnancies, and now, years later, I have confirmation that my instincts were on target. Does the developing baby get input from the outside before being born? By the time you get to the end of this story, you will know the answer.

Our seventh child came at a time when Jack and I were parents of three boys and three girls. Of course the boys were rooting for a baby brother, and the girls were hoping for a little sister, each side hoping to give their gender the edge. That seventh baby was born in 1968, years before ultrasound. Nobody knew for sure what sex the baby would be or what color baby clothes to buy.

Naming the baby became a family affair. "Yuck, we can't name a girl Linda. That's the girl who sits next to me at school. She has cooties," said Tim, with the conviction of an eight-year-old boy.

"Don't name a boy Michael," said Diane. "A Michael sits next to me and he's always in trouble. I wouldn't want a brother named Michael."

"I like Bruce," said Jack. "That's a good name for a Scot; he could be Bruce Stewart."

"Yeah, but Bruce was our dog who got killed when a truck hit him. That shouldn't be a baby's name," said Nancy, our oldest child. "I remember how bad we felt when Bruce died."

The list of names on the bulletin board grew longer and was constantly being reviewed and rejected. "I think we do have a name for a boy," I said. "What about Philip Andrew? We'll call him Andy. Both are good strong names." The girl's name was still up in the air as my due date came and went. In desperation we came up with a name. "If it's a girl, maybe we could name her after the town where she will be born, Marietta Georgia." Everyone groaned and complained, but had no better names for a little girl.

I was a few days overdue and we all were eager to get this new sibling here. Jack and I decided to go see the hot movie of June 1968, *The Graduate,* starring Anne Bancroft and Dustin Hoffman. We both knew it would be quite awhile before we could get out to a movie once the new baby was here. We saw the movie a few days before I gave birth. *The Graduate* remains high on my personal list of the hundred best movies of all time. The music of Simon and Garfunkel from the movie still appeals to me and I play it often.

Finally the big day came and I went into labor. Andy was a robust 9 pounds, 13 ounces, my largest child. When Daddy announced the new sibling was a brother, the boys cheered. The girls cried at their loss. Luckily we didn't have to choose a girl's name. To this day, as adults, all the children agree that Marietta Georgia would have been an awful name for a little girl.

Even though the girls were behind in numbers, they were always the ones up at 2:00 A.M. wanting to feed Andy. He fit in the family and grew in age and wisdom until he was ready to go off to college. "I want to go to Clemson," said Andy. He followed two of his siblings to this South Carolina university. He graduated and married his college sweetheart, Melanie.

Andy turned thirty-seven years old in 2005. His birthday coincided with Father's Day that year, June 19. Jack and I were celebrating Andy's birthday and Father's Day with Melanie and their children, Jackson and Emily.

The subject came around to movies we enjoyed. Anne Bancroft had just passed away and Melanie was telling me about the movie, *The Graduate,* that she and Andy watched every year while they were in college. "I just realized I'm the age that Anne Bancroft was in that movie, and she played the older woman! That makes me feel old," said Melanie.

When Andy and Melanie were students at Clemson University, the school showed *The Graduate* at the end of every school year. "We saw it every year. I guess we saw it six or seven times," said Melanie. "Andy wouldn't think of missing it."

That story triggered memories I had from thirty-seven years ago. I told her: "I saw that movie just a few days before Andy was born. Do you think that had anything to do with his fascination with *The Graduate?*"

Until then, I had no idea that Andy and his future wife had watched the same movie seven times as he finished his college work and became a landscape architect.

Back to the question whether an unborn baby is influenced by outside sounds. I'd have to say that Andy had a connection to *The Graduate* before he was born. It carried over into his life as a college student.

The following is for mothers-to-be. Think about that as you

experience your pregnancy and wait for the arrival of your child. As a fetus Andy heard music from that movie I watched. I like to think that songs like "The Sound of Silence" and "Scarborough Fair" got through the placenta barrier and helped make him the fine young man he is today.

What movies do you watch? What music does your developing baby hear? That new life does hear your music. Recent studies confirm that between five and six months the fetus hears its first sounds, the cacophony of its mother's body. The baby does respond to music vibrations heard in the womb.

Hearing Mozart might just have a different effect than hearing the likes of Eminem and assorted American Idol superstars.

Check it out for yourself. Sit quietly at a time when you feel active movements of your baby. Try a variety of music: hard rock, soothing lullabies, classical tunes. See how that baby responds.

Being pregnant is such a special time and choosing the best sounds for that new life to hear is so easy to do. Check the music you listen to on your CDs. Think about making a change for your baby's sake. Your child just might end up with the wonderful qualities Andy has!

Three Dog Night in Concert

The first rock concert Jack attended was Three Dog Night in Atlanta in 1973. He was clueless about what would happen. Son Tom asked, "Dad, would you go with the guitar group from church to see Three Dog Night? We need a chaperone and someone to drive us."

Keeping a teenager interested in participating in church services was high on his list of priorities. "Sure, I can get you all in the van."

The church had provided tickets and these teens were delighted to see where they would sit, three rows from the stage. Jack noticed speakers on both sides of them. They were stacked three high; each speaker was ten feet tall and six feet wide.

The opening act was T. Rex, trying for the big time. "I don't think they ever made it. The noise was far louder than the whistle on the Queen Mary, decibels above what the human ear can tolerate. The lead guitarist gyrated all over the stage and closed with bashing his guitar against the stage, smoke rolling and sparks flying, completely destroying a perfectly good electric guitar," he said. He thought the bank of speakers destroyed his hearing.

"I guess I heard Three Dog Night, but it took several tunes before my ears cleared up enough to appreciate 'Joy to the World.' 'Jeremiah was a bullfrog' barely penetrated my hearing," he said.

All the way home, the excited kids raved about how cool that music was. Jack was trying to get enough hearing back to navigate the traffic back to the Atlanta suburb where we lived. By the next day, he could hear well enough to listen to Tom telling his brothers and sisters about what a great night he and his group had.

Tom and his friends were enthusiastic about going to another concert like this. "If they give us tickets again, will you take us?"

Jack said, "I pretended I had lost all hearing. I still can't hear a thing. My old ears can't take this anymore. Maybe you can get one of *your* mothers or dads to take you next time."

What Shall I Do with the Palms?

"What shall I do with the palms?" Susie asked this question in all sincerity. "Aren't we supposed to burn them or something? Sister Mary Margaret told us you're never supposed to throw them in the trash with garbage."

What to do with the palms? How to pack to leave the U.S. for a year in France? Can I learn enough French? Why did I take three years of Latin in high school and no French and end up going to live in France twenty years later? Good questions, all, but the answers weren't there for me. So I decided to get on with the job ahead.

Jack was already in France in his new job. We were getting ready to move as soon as school was out. Nancy was graduating from high school in May. The other six children were finishing up their school year. We would be ready to move June 6, 1974, D-Day.

"Susie, I don't care what Sister Mary Margaret said. She isn't getting ready to put her furniture in storage and move to France," I said. "Put your palms in a plastic bag and put it in a box to store. While you're doing that, collect everyone else's and store them too. God will forgive us."

If you don't understand this dilemma, you aren't alone. The parish priest solemnly blessed these palms on Palm Sunday, a Catholic rite that commemorates the occasion. We store them for a year on a sacred picture and obsess about to how to dispose of them next year.

Moving to a foreign country was foreign to me. I had moved several times in America, but moving to France would be a new experience.

The children were not as enthusiastic as Jack. "Why can't Dad get a job in Atlanta, where he already works?" I heard this question more times than I care to remember.

"This is a great opportunity for him and for all of us," I said. "We'll be able to learn a new language and travel to really neat places, like Paris." I was having my own doubts, but didn't think it was a good idea to share this with these seven children. At eighteen, Nancy had just graduated from high school, John, seventeen, was to be a senior in the fall, Tom, sixteen, a year behind, Susie, fourteen, ready to start high school, Tim, thirteen, in middle school, Diane, eleven, in fifth grade, and Andy, six, ready to go to first grade.

Jack took a new job in preference to moving to Arizona and traveling back to the Southeast to cover the territory he now did from Atlanta. Besides, Michelin Tire Company would move this family to France, put us in a furnished house and give us a living allowance. From France we would eventually live in South Carolina. This wasn't a selling point to the kids either.

Before he left, Jack, the children and I got passports for everyone. We got medical records and shots up to date. Everyone got any needed dental care. I wasn't ready to trust my teeth to a dentist who didn't speak my own language.

Jack went to France the week after Easter. The rest of us stayed in Atlanta until after Nancy's graduation from Osborne High School. In those four weeks we had to prepare ourselves and our home for a move. Each person was allowed twenty kilos of airfreight to ship to France. That amounts to forty-four pounds. By the way, we had to start using the metric system even before we left home. Almost daily someone would put his or her box of treasures on the scale to see how much more to add. "I'll bring my tape player and tapes," said Tom. "If I bring those, everyone can use mine and not take another one."

"You have to have an adapter if you bring anything electrical," said Jack. "We'll buy some to make things work on 220-volt electrical circuits."

For the next month we packed and repacked until each of us decided we had the right stuff to survive in France for a year. We had suggestions from other expatriates who had been there already. "Bring toilet paper! The stuff here is awful. Bring a cookbook and measuring cups and spoons to cook with. Bring those books in English you've been wanting to read. Get phrase books and dictionaries for countries you may visit."

I didn't realize how important this last suggestion was until we had to tour Italy with a French-Italian phrasebook, and we didn't know either language.

Moving day arrived. Friends Bill and Irma Boltman took us to the airport and agreed to keep our Dodge van for us. That way we'd have a car when we got back home in a year or so.

Traveling with seven children is a monumental task. Irma had connections with the airline and arranged for someone to meet us in New York and get us to the right gate for the Air France flight to Paris. We would change there to another plane to Clermont-Ferrand, our final destination.

I breathed a sigh of relief once we were in the air. For the past week, the kids' friends came for last visits. I had an awful feeling someone would bail out and not be on the plane. But all seven were with me as we boarded the Air France jetliner.

A French flight attendant came up to eleven-year-old Diane and asked her, "Why are you going to France?"

"My Dad has a new job and we have to go live there," Diane replied.

"Can you speak French?" was the next question.

"No."

"Well, it's time to start learning. Here's a magazine to read." She handed Diane a French language magazine. That encounter made me realize what my life would be like once I hit the streets of Clermont-Ferrand.

Our departure was delayed at least an hour in New York because of long lines of air traffic. I knew this was a bad omen. We had very little time to change planes at Orly Airport in Paris.

Meanwhile Jack was waiting for us in Paris. He had spent the night on a park bench. Mme. Doussant, the lady in charge of personnel, could not get him a hotel. He came to the departure gate for the next leg of our flight. We weren't there. The plane for Clermont-Ferrand had already left. Now what? He didn't know if we were on it or not. We weren't. We couldn't find the right gate and my limited French was no help in getting answers.

Now we were wandering around Orly Airport wondering what to do next. Nancy looked up and said, "There's Dad!" We were ecstatic.

It took a few minutes to figure out what we had done wrong. The plane landed late; I didn't know how to clear customs and we had another big problem. I had tagged our bags to Paris, not Clermont-

Ferrand. There were no more flights to our new hometown till two days later.

That meant we had to take a train and carry the baggage for all eight of us. For the next few hours we boarded the Metro subway lines until we got to the train station. Our youngest child, six-year-old Andy, had the same amount of luggage as everyone else. Each time we left a train and boarded another I had an awful vision of leaving someone at the stop. I counted heads at every Metro stop. Those doors close whether your baby is on the train or not!

We finally arrived at our new home and for the next year, I never once thought about those palms!

To accommodate the many American families, the company had an American school for half days. During the other half day the American children attended French schools. This was a challenge to the kids, the parents, and the French teachers.

It took thirty years to hear stories of what really happened in the French schools that my children attended. I asked for it when I suggested in 2005 that each now-adult child write a story about her/his experience. That's when I learned what really went on in France.

Our oldest child, Nancy, had been accepted at Georgia State University in Atlanta and wanted to go to college in America, not France. She told me years later her main reason for going to college was to get out of France and have a life away from her siblings. Nancy went back to Atlanta after two months in France and graduated from Georgia State with a degree in physical therapy.

Diane and Andy attended the local French elementary school. Both had problems with the language. Both solved the language barrier by copying lessons from their French seatmates.

Eleven-year-old Diane wrote about how she survived French school. She survived by a certain amount of cheating. Here is her story.

"I needed glasses at the time we moved to France but did not know it. The way I found out was, for me, rather humiliating and not my favorite memory. I had to sit next to a rather large, dark French girl named Fatima. Anyway, we sat pretty far in the back. My teacher liked to write spelling words on the board, and we were to copy them down. Later in the week we had oral *dictée* where she read the spelling words and we wrote them down. Well, I came into this way behind the game in several ways. First of all, I could not read the words on the board to spell them correctly, and secondly, not knowing a whole lot of French, I had no idea if I was spelling them right. So in comes the part of Fatima, who reigns in my mind as a French version of the Terminator or Attila the Hun. I tried to copy her paper as we wrote the words from the board, desperate to avoid the bad marks and disgust from my French teacher.

"Fatima had other ideas. If she was going to be morally compromised by someone copying from her, there had to be some payoff. She had her eye on my nice neatly sharpened American colored pencils, in contrast to her broken, short, chewed off ones. The bargain was struck; in exchange for use of my colored pencils, she would allow a certain amount of looking at her paper (never mind that Fatima couldn't spell either, and I was copying poorly spelled words.) If the occasion arose where I did not have the colored pencils out at the correct time, the threat of a beating by Fatima at recess was always in the back of my mind."

Andy was in the same school as Diane. He too survived by a certain amount of cheating. Here is his story.

"The first thing I remember about living in France was how to cheat effectively. What I lacked was any other knowledge of the language to do any 'real' learning; so I did what any red-blooded, free-market entrepreneurial American would do - I borrowed answers off the paper of my desk mate, Olivier.

"Looking back, I think Olivier must have thought I was going to whip his French ass if he didn't make with the homework answers. He didn't refuse, and I never insisted, but it was understood that when an assignment was handed out, I would wait patiently until he was done and then write down on my paper what he wrote on his. We both made it through first grade with flying colors."

Another child told her story and it too included cheating. It was a different sort, but amounted to fraud. Fifteen-year-old Susie wrote the following story.

"The mode of transportation was either by moped or the city bus. I would wait at the bus stop and pick up the discarded bus tickets. I learned (actually I'm sure someone showed this to me) that the dates on the tickets could easily be erased - therefore allowing me to use the ticket for my next ride - at no charge! We had to be on the alert, though, because often a ticket taker would get on the bus and go around checking to see if everyone had a ticket. Luckily, we never got caught! I don't know how many tickets I re-used, but between all of us Americans, the bus system lost a lot of money that year."

Tim was one child who saw the year in France as a positive experience. He bought himself a bike and explored the chateaux around the area. He wrote that the French experience helped him cope later when he traveled to other parts of the world where people were even more "different" than the French. After college, Tim served several years in the Peace Corps in the Philippines.

There were a few escapades that we heard about quickly.

John was seventeen at the time and enjoyed the fact that there was no school on Wednesday afternoons. As I found out later, "We would all go to town on Wednesday and meet up with the other American kids at the local pub. No one was over eighteen years old. Anyone that wanted to could buy wine, beer, or any alcohol as long as you had the money."

A note appeared on M. Stewart's desk. Four teenage Stewarts and several teens from other families had been allowed to bring their lunch from home and eat at the American school during the two-hour lunch break. Seems they had gone downtown on the bus and purchased wine for lunch, brought it back and consumed it at the school. That was a story we heard as soon as it happened. That meant that they had to come home to eat their lunch.

"Monsieur Stewart, your children have been rolling rocks down the hill from your house. I have a report that they hit someone's car down below and ruined the top," said Mme. Doussant, who was responsible for housing and school problems for the American ex-patriots in France. The *Deuxchevaux* is a small two-passenger French car with a cloth top. M. Stewart came home and confronted our seven children.

"Did you guys roll rocks down the hill and hit some Frenchman's car?" he asked.

"No, not us. I bet they blame us because we have the most kids of any American family," said Tom, the sixteen-year-old spokesperson for the group.

So Dad went to the personnel office to confront the lady in charge. "Don't blame the Stewarts just because we have more kids than anyone else," he said.

It took twenty years to hear the real story about the car caper. "Yes, we did roll rocks down the hill, but we didn't know they hit a car," said John, another culprit in the event.

The fun was being able to take this large family all over Europe. We traveled in a Volkswagen van. Often we drew a crowd of teenagers at parks where we ate lunch. Here was a German car with French license plates, full of English-speaking kids eating a watermelon. In Verona, Italy, we shared our lunch with a group of curious Italian and Portuguese teenagers. They tried French with our kids, but resorted to English once they realized how bad our French was. It made me aware of how deficient we Americans are in foreign languages!

Michelin gave us a wonderful perk, a trip to Grandma's home in America for Christmas. When Jack picked up the tickets for us, there were only seven from Paris to the U.S. "We need eight tickets. There's no ticket for Andy," he said to Madame Doussant. "If he doesn't have a ticket, he'll have to stay with you while we're gone."

That got Madame Doussant's attention. "I know him; he cries!" Madame Doussant was familiar with six-year-old Andy. She had the task of getting him settled in French school. For the first week, he cried every day. She got him a ticket the next day.

The next hassle was that Michelin personnel folks considered Atlanta our home base. Nancy was there, in college, but no other family. We had to persuade them that Missouri, where Grandma lived, was our family home. We finally got approval to fly to Kansas City. Nancy flew in from Atlanta and met us there.

Getting nine people from the airport to Grandma's house forty miles away was the next challenge. Aunt Marie and Uncle Paul came with two station wagons to carry us to Grandma's. The four boys rode with Uncle Paul. On the way, they begged him, "Please stop at McDonald's. We haven't had a decent hamburger for six months!" Paul complied, and made buddies of his four nephews.

We got settled in at Grandma's house and were ready for bed after the long trip home. Jet lag set in. At 6:00 A.M. the next day all the children were bouncing on beds, joyfully looking at the six inches of snow out the window.

Shopping was high on our list. We came to the U.S. with empty suitcases, planning to load up on American underwear and Levi's jeans. My list included peanut butter. In France, peanut butter is a gourmet item, with a gourmet price. I went back to France with a twenty-pound case of peanut butter. Our family finished off that peanut butter by Valentine's Day!

It was a wonderful week with Grandma, cousins and friends. The children enjoyed hearing English spoken everywhere and insisted on seeing American movies, in English.

Sadly, we had to return to France after New Year's Day for the next six months.

We celebrated another Christmas holiday in France when we got back. The French have a big celebration on the feast of the Epiphany, January 6, "King's Day" as they call it. The King's Cake is the special treat for Epiphany. One person will find a toy baby in the cake. That person gets to wear a crown for the meal. It was a second Christmas, sort of a compensation for having to come back to a foreign country.

We decided to cut a tree from the nearby chateau. Tom tells the story of cutting our own Christmas tree. Jack and the four boys set out toward an abandoned chateau nearby. After several hours of struggle with cutting and carrying a tree, it was getting late.

As Tom tells it, "By this time it was dark, we were lost, had run out of food and water, and hauling a tree that seemed like it would fit better in Rockefeller Center. Tim and Andy found a stream and fell in. We made it home. The only problem was it was too high for the living room by about 3 feet. Dad brought in a power saw and trimmed things to fit. I must admit, that was the best damn Christmas tree I have ever seen."

The Stewarts' year was a challenge; it was also a fun time. The challenges were, naturally the language, a houseful of children who didn't really want to be there, and the hassles of a new culture, foods and French schools. We went as a family and survived living in a foreign country and adapting to a new language and a new way of life. The children were mostly teenagers by then. That brought plenty complaints, both from the children and from the schools. But again, we did survive and get back to American life.

We are all back to life in America and can look at the stories and laugh. It was a once-in-a-lifetime experience, one we agree wasn't all bad. The best part was that it lasted only one year instead of the two to three years the company originally proposed.

And now, thirty years later, I am still learning from my children what really went on in France! And those palms? They showed up when I unpacked my kitchenware in South Carolina. There they were in the bottom of a cookie jar. I still don't know what to do with them.

The Longest Toe

I first became aware of the toes in the Webster family when I heard my mother say about my Uncle Tom Webster, "His toes are so long they look like fingers." Uncle Tom was my Dad's brother and lived far away, so I didn't get a look at his toes while I was a child.

Just imagine an eight-year-old asking her uncle, "Let me see your toes, Uncle Tom." No way in my family.

When the Websters had their first reunion ever, in 1988, I planned a family activity. Because of this, I got my chance to see Uncle Tom's toes. The contest was to find the longest toe. Everyone with Webster blood in his/her veins shed a shoe and presented his/her longest toe.

I set up this contest with some hope of winning. My Dad wore size 13 shoes. Since I wasn't sure just how big Uncle Tom's feet were, I fantasized how these two brothers must have played together as children. Did they have contests with their feet to see who could make the biggest splash in a puddle after a summer rain? Did they toss a basketball back and forth with toes that were as long as fingers? Sadly, Dad died and was never a contestant in the contest. Uncle Tom won that first contest, toes down, 2-1/2 inches long. I was not even in the running.

After losing that first contest, I resolved to come back and win.

The Longest Toe

But fate would not be on my side. Complications from arthritis required that I have foot surgery. The surgery involved working on the bones of my feet. After the bandages came off, I looked closer at my repaired feet. The surgery had made my toes shorter. This was one possibility I had not considered. Jack measured my toes. Sure enough, the toes were a half-inch shorter than before. "You'll never equal Uncle Tom's record toe length!" he said.

By the next reunion five years later we had lost Uncle Tom. We all mourned his passing and remembered his toe length. This time his daughter Lois and my daughter Susan tied for first place in the longest toe contest. I am resigned to the fact that I will never win the longest toe contest at the Webster family reunion. Now it is in the hands, oops, toes of the younger generation.

Finding Michele

"**P**at, I want to find my baby," my sister sobbed over the phone. "Do you remember the attorney in Omaha who handled the adoption?"

Helen, my younger sister, as an unwed mother gave birth to a daughter in 1962. She came to live with us during her pregnancy. Jack and I had five preschoolers of our own, so we just set another plate at the dinner table. We helped her find an attorney and an obstetrician who would honor her request that the baby be put into a Catholic home. Helen delivered the baby, held her once in her arms, and let her go to another family.

Helen finished college, began a teaching career, married, and had two children. After thirty years, she began to want to see the child she gave away. When she called me in 1994, I had only one contact in the city where she gave birth. That contact was a friend of the attorney. He was of no help, retired and living in Arizona. Helen went to the modern source of help, the Internet. There she found a young lady searching for her birth mother. It turned out to be a match. Helen, now living in Houston, found Michele, living in Alabama, both far from Nebraska.

They arranged a meeting in Alabama. Helen broke the news to her family who were surprised, supportive and gradually came to know and love Michele and her family.

Michele is married and the mother of four wonderful children. Her life after adoption was not as planned. Her adoptive mother abandoned the family when Michele was very young. She was raised by her father with the help of her adoptive grandmother.

I wrote to Michele telling her of my part in her birth. I felt that she had already been a part of my family. It was an instant bonding for me.

Finding Michele and getting to know her family was an important milestone in Helen's life. She was blessed to be able to find the child she gave away and see what a remarkable adult the baby girl became.

In 2002 Michele lost the mother she had recently found. Helen was diagnosed with pancreatic cancer and died within a month. Michele traveled to be with her mother in her remaining days.

I recently received a letter from Michele saying, "I am sure glad that I met Helen and all of you. You make me feel like I have *always* been a part of the family! And what a great family!"

Michele and Helen not only found each other, I found a whole new branch of my family tree and want to "Keep in touch," as Michele said in closing her letter.

New Life Phases

Retirement is not a private affair. It is an intergenerational event that affects all the generations in your life and all its aspects. Jack and I were not thinking of retirement in 1995 when it was forced upon us. We had no burning desire for sleeping late, daily golf and bridge or world travel. We thought retirement was several years down the road.

As we entered this new phase of life, we were not prepared for the reality of life in retirement. It was not what you see in *AARP The Magazine*. Reality was resettling two elderly mothers, helping with two new grandchildren, one a very, very premature infant. We literally were nursing a newborn in South Carolina while tending to Jack's ninety-five-year-old mother in Seattle. With the help of son Tom in North Carolina, we relocated her to a nursing facility there.

Later that year my mother Margaret, age eighty-six, living in Missouri, called. "I just sold my house. Can you come help me clean it out? I have thirty days to move."

Margaret had been born in this house and my sisters and I grew up in there. I knew what a formidable task cleaning out her house would be.

For several years my sisters and I had badgered Mom to get rid of that house. It was a ten-room house, built in the 1870s and needing expensive maintenance and repairs. Her parents had purchased the house in April 1897. She sold it in March 1997.

Imagine this scenario. Margaret did not really want to move; she had never moved in her eighty-six years. My sisters had tried one summer to get her to "downsize" and get rid of some stuff. When one owns four sewing machines, closets of clothing from her family and others who left things when *they* died, it wasn't hard to figure this would be a monumental chore.

Jack started on the basement. He soon learned that if Mom was in on the process, nothing would get discarded. I took her to the clothing closets upstairs. He trashed box after box of old screws, canning jars, and stuff.

Mom went out on the porch and saw an ancient twenty-foot wooden extension ladder in the discard pile. "Don't throw that away! Bob, the handyman across the street can use it." The ladder was the one I saw lying under the porch as far back as I can remember. Mom resisted Jack's admonitions about safety and OSHA regulations.

Jack finally convinced Mom to give up the old ladder. He said, "Mom, that ladder is too dangerous for Bob or anyone else to climb. He'd probably break a rung and get killed when he falls."

Upstairs I tried to convince Mom to discard some of the thousands of sewing patterns she had. Some were for dresses I wore as a child sixty years ago! "I might need one of those someday." This was the standard reply I heard for the next few days.

Logic and our presence prevailed on her to keep one room for the things she could put into the senior apartment she would be moving into. Her most prized possession was an ancient "pie safe." This article of furniture dated back at least one hundred years. Jack had helped her restore it and it was a fine piece of furniture. It was the first piece the antique dealers wanted to buy. She held out and insisted on moving it. Two strong males had a hernia-producing time getting it into the small apartment.

All of us had to keep a close watch on the piles to give away. We found the old wooden picnic basket back in the "save" room time after time. "I know I'll need that basket when we go on picnics," Mom kept insisting.

My sister Mary Ann and her husband John helped with the final days of the move. I was grateful I did not have to be there when Mom left the house she was born in. Mary Ann told me, "As we drove away, Mom never looked back."

Months later I returned to Missouri to visit Mom in her new home. She now lives in downtown Kansas City. She can walk to daily Mass at the Cathedral next door. Mom told me of going to hear Dr. Joyce Brothers speak at the nearby Municipal Auditorium. "And it was free."

Recalling the struggle with the pie safe, I made a point of remarking how well it fit into such a small space. Mom's answer to me was, "Do you think Susie would like to have it?" (Susie is my daughter in South Carolina.) "I don't really have space for it. Jack helped me fix it up, so I thought Susie would like to have it."

As I ponder on these events from a later date, I realize how much we were asking of my mother. The house and its contents were her life. Her parents were German immigrants. Her father Remig came to America to avoid being drafted into the German army. Her mother Theresia left a tiny village where she worked in a cigar factory. In America Remig practiced his butcher's trade and became the owner of his own grocery store. Margaret was the heir of the legacy of hard work and dedication that came from her parents. As her daughter I see how the lives and times of these people shaped my life.

The odyssey just recounted is a litany of intergenerational triumph. Mom taught me about aging and planning for retirement. She left her home before she was too frail to care for it and herself. She has adapted to a new life in an apartment in a city near to her daughter, grandchildren and great-grandchildren. Jack and I, now in our seventies, are able-bodied and care for our home and ourselves. But as we age, I can see the value of adapting to a new way of life. I am grateful that my mother made the move. It was helpful for her. It will make the lives of her children less stressful knowing that she is in a safe place. I intend to do the same for my children.

Sentimental Memory Books

What does a mother do with over thirty-three years of accumulated memorabilia from raising seven children? I was determined to clean out some of this accumulated "junk" a few years ago. Jack was doing some research on a paper he was writing to document his claim to know something about marriage and the family. He began by digging out our marriage certificate, located each child's birth certificate, then continued to find the date of their baptism, First Communion, confirmation, and in some cases, marriage. As he got what he needed, I got more and more involved with a trip down memory lane.

Needless to say, with seven children our collection was extensive. I did not want to keep *all* that stuff. But when I came across a hand-made Mother's Day card with two dimes taped to it and the message, "Spend this on yourself, not on us kids," I couldn't throw such a treasure away.

A friend solved the problem when she showed me a memory book her mother had made for her. This mother had decided to really clean out stuff when she and her husband retired and moved to a small apartment. That gave me the inspiration I needed.

I went out and bought seven albums, the loose-leaf kind with plastic pages. I started each one out with the hospital birth certificate.

I put in any clippings from the local newspaper, telling of that child's birth. The best school papers were included. One son asked, "Why didn't you put in those detention notes from my calculus teacher?" Since he wanted it, and since I still had it, he got it. I put in as many school pictures as I thought the recipient could handle.

Each child received a copy of "The Rules of the House." These were written rules, posted on the bulletin board for at least fifteen years. A list of job assignments changed from year to year to reflect changing job responsibilities, and the appropriate one went into each child's book.

Special pieces by each child included poetry, stories, and, best of all, handmade cards for every occasion. Dad and Mom's birthdays were big events. Mother's and Father's Day cards were priceless gifts. One enterprising son had priced each card on the back. Many had coins taped on the card to "buy something for yourself." Hallmark can never hope to compete with these entrepreneurs.

As the years went by, graduation announcements appeared, then wedding invitations. Jack was still caught up in his pursuit of a college degree at his advanced age, so he did not have time to get very involved with the memory book project. He glanced at one of the books one day, and exclaimed, "You're not going to give away all this good stuff, are you?" That had been my plan all along, to clean out some of the accumulated boxes. That is when I had to buy an eighth memory book, for him. He didn't want all the things from all seven kids, just selected pieces. We compromised and compressed his souvenirs into one book.

In all, this took most of a winter to do. I had thought I would give them as Christmas gifts for the next year. But I decided against that. I thought it would be more meaningful if each child could enjoy the scrapbook with no other siblings present. Son John and his children were visiting when I gave him the first book. John's children loved the book and they got a kick out of seeing their father's old papers and pictures.

This was truly a labor of love, one I would recommend at any stage of your child's life. As I did the books for my children, I came across grandchildren's papers. Now I have a collection box for them too. I just may never get rid of all that stuff.

I Would Never Do That!

Does something happen to parents when they become grandparents? Visiting grandchildren caused me to assess my "I would never do that!" stance on two subjects. I'll never buy sugared cereal and I'll never stand in line to buy a new kid product.

My cardinal rule was that "If you see it advertised on Saturday morning television, don't ask me to buy it." Cereals were mega advertisers. That translated into higher prices. I raised my children under that onerous cloud of deprivation. They ate the wholesome unsugared cereals like Wheaties, corn flakes and oatmeal. Since then I have learned there was sugar hidden in those cereals too. But that was before the nutrition labels!

My daughter Susie saw a box of cereal I had for the visiting grandchildren. Her four-year-old Taylor wanted some of those Reese's Puffs, the ones with Hershey's Cocoa and Reese's Peanut Butter Sweet & Crunchy Corn Puffs.

"I can't believe you have cereal like this. You never bought this kind of cereal for us when we were kids!" she said. "We had to eat those dull and boring cereals you always bought."

"I guess you caught me. I got it on sale at the store with a coupon," I said.

"Yeah, my Mom doesn't buy that kind for me," said Taylor. "Mom wants me to eat stuff like grits and eggs, not good cereal like that. I like it when Grandma buys me great cereal."

All those years of not giving in to advertising for stuff kids really want sort of went out the door as I aged. I still rationalize that I buy only what is on sale and usually with a doubled coupon.

But in the back of my mind I hear this voice saying to me, "I swore I'd never do that!" Never say never.

I got hit with another never. As I stood in line June 7, 2000, at midnight with hundreds of others at the local bookstore, I had a feeling of déjà vu. I resisted the pleas of children for forty-five years to go to Disney World. I do not stand in lines waiting to pay $45 for a chance to ride carnival rides.

So why would I go shopping at this ridiculous hour? The answer is Harry Potter. My grandson Stewart is one of those millions of kids who had been eagerly waiting for the newest book in this series. The marketing for this book even got to me. The publishers did not reveal its title until a few days before publication. *Harry Potter and the Goblet of Fire,* 734 pages long and priced at $25.95, is a writer's dream. The public address system announced a 40% discount on Potter's book.

Eager buyers could line up at the store from 11:00 P.M. on, but under no circumstances could they buy books until one minute past midnight July 8. Stewart was visiting from Atlanta and I agreed we'd go stand in line and be one of the first to buy it.

Clerks rushed around in wizard hats. Little Harry wanna-bes wore costumes and had the mark of the lightning on their foreheads. It became infectious as the witching hour approached. It was like New

Years' Eve. The countdown began, ten, nine, etc., until the lucky person at the head of the line got to put down her $15.57, plus tax.

As an avid reader myself, I am thrilled when my children and grandchildren want to read *anything*. I will buy them books before I'd buy toys or clothes.

We drove Stewart back to Atlanta the next day. As we handed him back to his mother, I asked him, "What page are you on?"

"Page 175, but I'll finish it tomorrow or the next day," he said.

Was it worth it? Why would I do something like this when I could just go buy the book the next morning?

Seeing children and adults get excited about reading is why. It excites me too, and if it takes the story of an orphan boy coming of age in the Hogwarts School of Magic, I will stand in line to buy that book to get young people reading.

I have to confess. In that one week, I did two things I swore I'd never do. "The grandchildren made me do it!"

The Circle of Life

Ecclesiastes chapter 3 says it all:
For everything there is a season,
and a time for every matter under heaven:
A time to be born, and a time to die;

This month, as always, one life ended and a new one began. In itself that is not unusual; it is the circle of life everywhere. But I have never experienced it as I did in the month of June 2001.

Life ended for Colonel Winston Wallace, my daughter-in-law's grandfather. The Colonel came into my life ten years ago when my son Andy married his granddaughter Melanie.

a time to plant, and a time to pluck up what is planted;

The Colonel joined our annual family tomato contest. It has become a real challenge with the branches of the family vying to produce the first and largest tomato. The losers give the winner a six-pack of his/her choice. The winner gives a party to receive the six packs.

a time to kill, and a time to heal;

The Colonel had consistently won the prize for the first tomato of the season. That year his plants produced the first tomato on June 8. At that time he was seriously ill. He died several weeks later. It is ironic that a dying man won the contest over all the younger family gardeners. I later understood his advantage when I read his obituary. He had a B.S. in Agricultural Education from Virginia Polytechnic Institute! He later taught agriculture in a Virginia high school.

Several years ago he shared one of his secrets for dealing with tomato cutworms. When he found these pests on his plants, he made an example of them. He stationed himself in front of his plants and executed the worm as a warning to any others who may have considered eating *his* tomatoes.

a time for war, and a time for peace.

I attended the full military ceremony for his burial. It was new to me—the flag-covered coffin, the six soldiers with rifles, firing three rounds in unison, a bugler playing "Taps," folding the flag and handing it to his widow. Very impressive. The lone piper playing "Danny Boy" in the background was a testimony to his Scottish heritage.

a time to weep, and a time to laugh;
a time to mourn, and a time to dance;

As the funeral service for the Colonel was happening here in South Carolina, in Georgia our granddaughter Theresa was in labor with her baby. The same day we put the Colonel to rest, a new life, baby Haley Monique, our great-granddaughter came into the world.

Later that same week, another child in the Colonel's family was baptized in the same Presbyterian Church where his funeral service was held a few days earlier. Five-month-old Emily Mae, the Colonel's great-granddaughter, became the newest addition to the Colonel's church.

Of course these two little girls are not here to replace the Colonel, but new life happens and it is a testimony to the resilience of all families. Haley and Emily have all the potential for a life as full and rewarding in the twenty-first century, as did the Colonel, an educator and tomato grower from the twentieth century.

The circle was completed and new life goes on in the two little girls, newly born and newly baptized.

Helen, Rebel without a Cause

My younger sister Helen made a shrine to James Dean in her home. She had photos, stories, movie magazines, clippings and a life-size cutout of James Dean with his cigarette hanging from his fingers. You had to come from the era of *Rebel Without a Cause* and *East of Eden* to get Helen's fascination with this guy. No one in our family got him, just Helen. Her daughter Amy complained, "My picture never made it to the mantel. Neither did my children. We were relegated to a bookcase. Only James Dean got that place of honor."

At Helen's funeral the presiding priest commented that he was used to seeing flowers, pictures and grandchildren's scrawls in a sick person's room. "But I looked at the wall and there was James Dean." He felt that, like Jesus, Dean was a rebel and that was Helen's reason for her feeling of kinship with him. Perhaps.

Helen was truly the rebel in the family. She rebelled against going to first grade. She stayed home a few weeks rather than go to school. As her older sister, I was humiliated at Mom literally dragging her down the street to school.

"But," as Mom said later, "once she went to school, she never left." Indeed, she went to college, graduated with a teaching degree, and taught school until she became ill and died at age sixty-two.

Helen taught English literature to 180 high school seniors. She worked hard to make Macbeth and Robbie Burns interesting for them. She played tennis every Wednesday with a score of friends. She loved her children and grandchildren, had many friends and was glowing with life. She planned to retire in May 2002 and do the fun things she had delayed for years, travel and visit her family all over the country.

Jack and I slept with James Dean looking on whenever we visited her home in Houston. His presence dominated the guest room. Helen was teaching her classes at this time and appeared in excellent health.

At Houston's M. D. Anderson Cancer Center, tests confirmed that she had pancreatic cancer. They told her she was not a candidate for surgery. She was also too weak for chemo treatment. They recommended Hospice care. She railed at the physician's assistant who gave her this news. "You are just sending me there to die!" A few days later she was sent to Hospice at the Texas Medical Center. My sister Mary Ann who is a nurse called me to Houston to say good-bye to our sibling.

Hospice at this center is a unique experience. The family is able to be with the patient at all times. The staff makes it a point to do anything to make the family and patient comfortable. They gave medications, support, bedside time, counseling and caring. The building has a kitchen for family to store food and snacks. We took over a corner of the cabinets with plates, cups, fruit, peanut butter and drinks. We shared tears, food and death with other families staying with loved ones. When the atmosphere got overwhelming, I would go for a walk in the beautiful grounds with flower gardens and meditation space. The chapel was another haven for me.

When I arrived, Helen was lucid and knew who I was. I read to her from Flannery O'Connor, one of her favorite writers. At one point she told me, "Not so fast." I was used to reading to three-year-olds who would be restless when I slowed down. Helen wanted to slow down and hold on.

In her last days, her husband, two daughters and a son, our ninety-one-year-old mother, three sisters, Mary Ann, Kathleen and I, and two brothers-in-law surrounded Helen. We all took turns at round-the-clock shifts. She was never alone.

After her death, her daughter Amy arranged a funeral service with poetry and a favorite song from Sarah Brightman, "Time to Say Good-bye." James Dean attended the memorial service following the funeral. His life-size cardboard replica stood near the family photos. The English department from Hastings High School brought a meal for the two hundred people who attended. All wore a yellow rose. For an hour her fellow teachers and friends told stories of her love of life and her caring for her students.

She jokingly referred to me as "The Alpha Female" since I was the oldest. I still use that name as a pseudonym. At the memorial, one of her friends came up to me and said, "I was supposed to go to the beach with Helen last September, but she told me she couldn't. 'The Alpha Female is coming that weekend and I can't go with you.'"

I'm sorry her friend didn't get to Galveston with Helen, but I am so glad I had the opportunity to be with her for a last few days of fun and hanging out with James Dean.

I think about my sister as I knew her as a child growing up, going to college and becoming a teacher. She was the rebel in our family. At times I cringed at her pranks. She spied on my dates and me in high school. A favorite prank was feeding her son's boa constrictor at a

New Years' Eve party. First-time guests were appalled at the boa's meal of a live white mouse. Whenever I see an old movie starring James Dean I do not dwell on his charisma, but on his biggest fan, the rebel I knew as my sister Helen.

Voting in 2004

I am pleased to announce that my voting record has been kept intact. Since my first vote for president, for Adlai Stevenson in 1956, I have voted for every losing presidential candidate. My votes for Barry Goldwater and Gene McCarthy went for naught too. It became a stretch when I voted for a winner, John Kennedy, but my vote didn't count since the state of Nebraska electors chose Richard Nixon. My record stays intact after November 2, 2004. I must confess that I helped along the losing candidate in this election.

Jack and I went to Kansas City in October 2004 to help care for my ninety-three-year-old mother while my sister and her husband went on vacation. The newspaper ran stories encouraging everyone to get out and vote in the 2004 election. That October Missouri was considered a "swing" state and a few votes might help the right candidate win.

So I got revved up to get Mom her absentee ballot and send it in. The process was quite simple. I went to election headquarters and filled out a form to get her a ballot. As her daughter, I was allowed to fill in her data. Her reason for voting absentee was her incapacity because of illness.

Her ballot came in the mail a few days later. We looked at the formidable set of papers and groaned. With macular degeneration, there was no way she could read the fine print and punch out the tiny numbers of her candidates.

The kit included a tool to punch out the numbers and a Styrofoam backing to put behind the card. I had a hard time with it and I knew there was no way she'd ever see what to do. The first item on the ballot was for President.

But my dirty secret is what happened when I helped Mom. I helped her vote for the loser too. I didn't try to influence her; she chose to vote a straight Democratic ticket.

"Do you want me to help you do this? I'd know how you voted," I said.

"That doesn't bother me. Just read me the choices," she said.

"Who do you want to vote for?" I asked.

"I just want to vote a straight ticket. I don't want to bother with all those other pages. I don't know any of the local people."

So I punched the number 5 and went on to the questions about keeping judges in office. She voted for money for better roads and against a tax increase for a new sports complex. (I was happy to see a vote for better roads. In the 2,300 miles we traveled on that trip, the very worst roads were on I-70 from St. Louis to Kansas City.)

Before I put the ballot in the envelope, I checked the back for hanging chads, the nemesis of the 2000 election. Sure enough, I had to pull off several of those suckers to ensure her vote would count.

I was convinced that if the next president was elected because of the swing state votes, it would be because Margaret Webster got her absentee ballot and voted that straight ticket for John Kerry. But as we now know, that didn't happen. Now President Bush owes his election to Margaret Webster, who voted absentee in Kansas City. With the two of us voting for the loser, there was no way Bush could lose!

One last word of advice: if any of you ever run for elected office, be sure and tell me so I don't vote for you. My vote would ensure your loss!

The Songs of My Life

Getting ready to celebrate our 50th wedding anniversary in 2005, our children volunteered to make a DVD to show at our anniversary dinner. The DVD will have family pictures from the past fifty years. Accompanying the photos will be songs of the era, 1950s, 1960s, etc. Computer savvy children offered to put it all together once we selected pictures and songs.

Pictures were easy to find. All it took was going through thirty photo albums and 3000 slides! We spent a week at this activity. Our goal was to include every person invited to the party. Some were easy: children, grandchildren and great-grandchildren showed up in dozens of pictures. Old friends, not seen for years would have to be content to see themselves as we saw them last, some forty years ago.

How do you choose from a college graduation picture and one showing a child being goofy, just a child? How about four-year-old Andy in his Indian loincloth with a necklace of turkey bones around his neck? Or Susie and John holding their ears while Nancy practices her clarinet? Diane and Tom showed up with prom partners, long forgotten, in 1970s attire. Gross! An easy choice was one of Tim in a jeepney with a Clemson sticker on the bumper. This was taken while he served in the Peace Corps in the Philippines. Choosing the first group was the easy part; making the final cut was much more difficult. We tossed out all pictures of babies in the buff and any with gross eating shots.

Going through fifty years of slides is an exhausting project. They evoke memories from times both happy and sad. The happy times show the family as an ever-evolving entity with children in diapers, going off to school, dating, college-bound, and marriage. We see old family members who are no longer here with us. Friends who have passed on come to life again on the screen.

Grandchildren proved to be an eager audience for old slides. "Is that really my Mom? She sure looks goofy!" was a frequent comment. "Did my Dad really wear those dorky clothes and glasses?"

Choosing songs proved to be more difficult. Most choices required an old-style "record player" with a turntable. Fortunately, we still had our old stereo outfit that took 33-RPM and 45-RPM records. (Not many of those around anymore!) Our children were quick to tell us: "You can get all that old stuff by downloading it from the Internet. Just give us titles and the singer and we can find it." I hesitated to ask if they could possibly use those songs in the original format, the LP record. I knew the answer. I happened on a message on the Internet sent from Andy to Susie. Andy wants to use Cheap Trick's "Surrender" with the lyrics: "Mama's all right, Daddy's all right, they just seem a little weeeird!" I think I'd better come up with my own song selections for this project.

The children suggested one set of artists that both generations would enjoy, Simon and Garfunkel. I could agree with that. I'm not so sure about Andy's suggestion of "Mrs. Robinson" by the Lemonheads as a contrast to the original. But what to choose from all those winners from the early years? Our children won't want to hear the likes of

Rosemary Clooney, Eddie Fisher, Ernie Ford, or Julie Andrews.

I also intercepted a message between children suggesting making a postage stamp of their parents. Apparently you can go on-line and someone out there will create a stamp, approved by the USPS, with a photo on it. I wasn't sure I wanted our invitations going all over the country with a caricature of Jack and me on the envelope. But they did.

We didn't have a big fancy wedding. The day of our wedding, February 5, 1955, it snowed fourteen inches. We were lucky to get to the church and many guests didn't venture out till the afternoon reception. We spent our honeymoon in our small apartment. I've read a factoid that the length of a marriage is inversely proportional to the cost of the wedding. More money spent, less years married. Surviving fifty years in a relationship does have its merits. I like to think that is how it worked for us. $20,000 today can be an average wedding cost. Seems the average length of a marriage is much less than any fifty years. The cost of our wedding barely reached three figures. I guess staying together fifty years compensates for that frugal wedding day!

So what songs did end up representing our fifty years together? These songs were included in our anniversary DVD: "Ave Maria" by Sarah Brightman, "Blowin' in the Wind" by Peter, Paul and Mary, "The Sound of Silence" by Simon and Garfunkel, "Joy to the World" by Three Dog Night, and "Rhythm of My Heart" by Rod Stewart. These are truly the songs of my life.

Jack's Stories

After fifty years of marriage, I have learned a lot about the man who came into my life in 1955. He likes to tell this story about his earliest memory of going to the hospital.

* * *

Little Jackie was sick. He hurt in his belly. His Mom finally called Dr. Hartigan to come check out her four-year-old son. Dr. Hartigan drove to the house and found Jackie on his parent's bed. The chenille bedspread had left tracks on his cheeks.

"Let's see what's wrong with this boy," the doctor said. He poked at Jackie's belly, but found no sign of a problem. "Does this hurt?"

"No," Jackie said, "not there." Doctor Hartigan kept poking and checking the patient's vital signs. "Are you sure this part of your belly doesn't hurt when I press it?" he asked.

Jackie kept insisting, "Nothing hurts." Still his Mom knew something was wrong.

"He's been peaked all day, just looks wan and sickly," she said.

The doctor picked up his bag and stethoscope and turned to go out the door. He started down the porch steps. But then he came back to the bedroom. "I'm going to have one more look at that boy." He poked even harder into Jackie's belly.

Jackie howled. "I just can't take it any more!"

"Is this where it hurts? I think this boy has a case of appendicitis," said Dr. Hartigan. "We need to get him to Sisters' Hospital for surgery."

Jackie woke up after having his appendix out at the hospital. He still hurt and saw his Mom and Dad in the room.

"I'm glad to see you're awake now. You had us worried for awhile," said his Dad. "I brought you a present to help keep you company while you get well." It was a gray Easter bunny with pink ears. He put the bunny in bed with Jackie.

"Thank you Dad," said Jackie. "That's a nice present and next Sunday will be Easter. I'll take him to church with me."

"I don't think you'll be able to go to church on Easter," said Mom. "That's only a few days away. You'll need to stay home and rest."

Jackie went home and recovered in a few weeks. The scar was a worry to him. "When will it go away?"

The doctor assured him it would be much smaller as he got older. One day Jackie decided to give his bunny a scar just like his. He got his mother's sewing kit and went to work. He made an incision in a place on the bunny where his own scar was. He took out some stuffing and sewed up the bunny's appendix incision. "Now the bunny has a scar just like me."

That little boy is now my husband Jack, and his scar is still there from that appendectomy years ago. It did not shrink; it got bigger.

* * *

As an adult Jack tells how his specific gravity is greater than one, and that is why he cannot swim. He dictated this story to me and I wrote it in his voice. PWS

I don't know how to swim. I sink like a rock. My body density is greater than one, so I am too dense to float. My wife says I have lead in my ass. That's why I don't swim and I don't intend to learn.

My non-swimming career began the summer my mother sent me to the Municipal Pool to learn how to swim. "I have to work all day and you don't have anything better to do now that school is out. I'm signing you up for swimming lessons at the pool. You can walk there every day and have the lessons."

The pool was only a few blocks from my house and in those long gone days an eight-year-old boy could walk anywhere in my small town. There were no predators, and very few cars. Gas rationing of the World War II era kept casual driving to a minimum. One didn't spend precious gas coupons to drive children around who were perfectly able to walk to a fun place like the local swimming pool.

I took Mom's $2.50 and went to sign up for lessons. I had never been in a swimming pool before and was ready for almost anything. What I got was not what I expected. Dick, the teenage lifeguard, stood on the deck of the pool. The sun was up, but in early June the morning air wasn't all that warm yet. Ten of us waited to hear what to do next. I started to shiver.

"First we jump in the shallow end. Grab the side of the pool, stretch out and kick. Get your face in the water and blow bubbles," said Dick. That was easy enough and I relaxed a little. This swimming was no big deal. After a few minutes in the shallow water, Dick blew his whistle.

"Now let's go to the deep end and start to swim. Jump in and go to the side," said the lifeguard. "That's when you learn to swim."

I followed the crowd to the deep end. "10 feet" the sign read. I jumped in and found myself on the bottom of the pool. My feet felt concrete below me and I saw only water around me. I had no idea what to do next, but I knew I had to do it quick. I didn't have my glasses on and couldn't see very far in front of me. Besides, all there was to see was water. I walked a few steps and finally saw what appeared to be a ladder in front of me. Still walking on the bottom of the pool, I grabbed the ladder and started climbing. I got out of that pool, went in the dressing room and changed my clothes. I went home and never looked back.

I didn't tell my mother that I skipped the rest of the swimming classes and she never asked me how I was doing. She went to work every day, assuming that I was learning to swim. To the end of her days at age ninety-six, I never told her I wasted that $2.50 she paid the pool for lessons.

To this day I am not a swimmer. If I go in the water, I stay where I can touch the bottom with my head out of the water. My wife and children love to swim and have progressed from the minnow level through fish, shark and flying fish. Me, I stay at the side of the pool and cheer them on. My career as a swimmer ended the day I walked across the bottom of the pool to the safety of a ladder where I could get air into my lungs. And never go back. I never forgot the feeling I had as I walked on the bottom of that pool. I truly could be called a rock with legs.

* * *

"Stop dragging your feet, Jackie, and let's get home. After we have dinner, we're going to see Grandma and Aunt Anna."

Every Sunday after 10:00 o'clock Mass and dinner, ten-year-old

Jackie and his Mom visited Grandma and Aunt Anna. There was no way out.

"Even on a nice day like today, I have to go read to Grandma and hear her stories. I'd rather be out riding my bike and seeing what Kyle is doing. We could go fishing and catch frogs."

Jackie was dispatched to his grandmother's upstairs bedroom while his Mom and Aunt Anna spent the afternoon gossiping about the family. "That Jarvis is still as strange as ever. He teaches art at some college a thousand miles away. I guess he still has that awful beard," said Jackie's Mom. "And he never sends his mother anything, not even a handkerchief, for Mother's Day!"

Mom didn't like her late husband's brother, Jarvis, the artist. Jackie had seen some of Uncle Jarvis' work and thought it wasn't so bad. The best one was the picture they hung upside down in the art show at the museum. When Jarvis saw it, he said, "You numskulls, take it down and hang it right." In 1948 in the little Midwestern town, folks didn't much appreciate modern art and modern artists.

"He was the original beatnik, wearing sandals and that shaggy beard," said his family. He predated the hippies of the 1970s by thirty years.

"Jarvis was bad enough, but what about that wife of his, Madge?" Aunt Anna's favorite subject was Madge and her peculiar ways. "She always was strange. She made that ugly pottery she called fine art. We were all glad that they lived so far away."

Every Sunday Jackie heard the same stories. One story was a mystery. When Mom and Aunt Anna talked about Aunt Bessie, their voices dropped to a whisper.

Aunt Anna said, "You know how she was, always running after

the boys. We had to put her in a convent in Denver." Jackie strained to hear the rest of the story, but for all his life he wondered about that convent in Denver where another aunt lived. Did she become a nun? Jackie's contact with nuns was as the teachers at St. Joseph's school. It was still mysterious and no one would tell him where Bessie lived.

Jackie's job at Grandma's was to write letters for her and check to see what else she might need. "I hope she doesn't want me to comb her hair!" he thought. She was frail, bedfast from the ravages of Parkinson's disease. Her hands shook a lot, and she couldn't write well anymore. Jackie tried to keep the visits as short as possible. While his mother and aunt talked on and on, he was trapped in Grandma's bedroom.

Her room was a clean, bright sunny room and had lilacs from the yard in a vase. He could smell the lilac bushes outside the open window. To this day, the fragrance of lilacs puts Jack back in Grandma's bedroom.

Jackie's tactic was to stand as near to the door as he could without appearing too rude. "I like to stand here where there's always a breeze," said Jackie. It was also a convenient place to make a quick exit as soon as Grandma closed her eyes and began to doze off.

Today, however, she had a chore for Jackie. "I want you to write down a poem I have in my head. I call it 'Picture of a Saint.' But my hands are so shaky I can't write anymore. I know how well you do in school. So I want you to write down the poem for me. I'll say it slowly and make sure you spell all the words correctly."

She began to dictate the poem and Jackie had no trouble writing the words since she talked so slowly. "Read it back to me and let me hear how it sounds. Change that phrase from 'My God, why have you forsaken me?' You had the words wrong." She finished and closed her eyes. Jackie backed a few steps into the doorway. "Don't forget to keep that poem and remember me when you read it."

"Of course, Grandma. I think I hear my Mom calling me. It's time to go home. Bye, Grandma."

On the way home, Mom asked Jackie, "Did you have a nice visit with your Grandmother? I know she likes having you come see her. She gets lonely up there."

"Sure, she usually has a story to tell me. Today she dictated a poem. I wrote it down and she wants me to keep it."

Jackie grew up, became Jack and went away to college. While he was away, Grandma died. "I'm sorry I don't have the money to come back for Grandma's funeral. I wish I could. I still have her poem," he told his mother.

"Jarvis and Madge were there, peculiar as always, but at least they came to the funeral," Jack's mother said.

Fifty years later Jack went through his files and found Grandma's poem. All those years faded away in an instant.

He was Jackie again, standing near the door, ready to leave his grandmother's room. "I had this feeling of sadness and guilt as I read her poem. I'm going to send it to Catholic Digest and see if they will publish it. Maybe that way she'll still be here with us."

The magazine ignored the submission. Jack still keeps the poem and tells his grandchildren about their great-grandmother's poem. It is his way to keep her memory alive. It is indeed the "Picture of a Saint."

Picture of a Saint

Early one summer morning while attending Mass
A dark-robed priest knelt in prayer.
His face held visions.

At times he seemed in bodily pain
As he looked towards the crucifix
Living over the death of Christ on the cross.

And a look of fear came into his eyes
As though he heard the words
"My God, My God, why hast Thou forsaken me?"

Then, a look of humility as he heard the words
"Forgive them, Father, they know not what they do."
Then he looked towards the stained windowpane.

But in spirit he was over the rugged mountains
Far over the deep blue sea
Walking and talking to the Man of Galilee.

Then a stream of sunlight came through the window
Making a halo over his bowed young head.
The light came in like a burst of music chanting the Great Amen.

I long to be an artist that this picture I could paint
And when finished I would write beneath on canvas
This is the picture of a saint.

When Jack was a teenager, he had his fifteen minutes of fame. He says he was the "hottest flier" in the model airplane championship in Detroit. No, he wasn't a World War II flying ace. He was a fifteen-year-old, flying model airplanes in the International Model Airplane Contest.

Jack's most exciting moment came when the handkerchief in his pocket caught on fire. He had used his handkerchief to snuff out the fuse on a timing device, which serves to help bring the planes down after they have been up for the allotted time. He stuffed the handkerchief in his pocket and went back to his business.

A short time later spectators and contestants were amazed to see young Stewart strolling casually while smoke billowed from his hip pocket. After a hasty warning he yanked the smoking handkerchief out of his pocket and found two silver-dollar sized charred holes in it. Stewart now held the distinction as being the "hottest flier" among the five hundred contestants.

"I thought it was getting kind of hot back there, but I couldn't figure out what was causing it," he commented, looking at his scorched handkerchief. To this day Jack has that holey souvenir.

Jack was always fascinated with building and flying model planes. Fifteen-year-old Jack Stewart was one of five hundred selected from thousands to participate in the International Model Airplane contest in Detroit in 1951. The Dodge-Plymouth Motor dealers in St. Joseph, Missouri sponsored him and paid his travel and hotel bill in Detroit.

It was an exciting trip for Stewart who had never been to a big city like Detroit. He was an avid model builder and competed in several contests to qualify to go to Detroit. Two other teenagers from his hometown went too. They flew free-flight planes and jet planes. One plane had a wingspan of eight feet. To get their planes and equipment to Detroit, they had a unique solution. A local mortuary provided a casket crate to carry on top of the car they drove. The driver was the Plymouth dealer in St. Joseph, the sponsor of the competition. Along with the three boys and the dealer was the sports writer for the *St. Joseph News Press and Gazette*. He filed two reports daily to the papers back home. Stewart financed his plane costs by working as a *News-Press and Gazette* carrier salesman.

A highlight of his trip was seeing the Detroit Tigers vs. New York Yankees, the first major league baseball game for Jack. He watched Yogi Berra and Johnny Mize hit home runs against the Tigers. "This will be something to tell my grandchildren about," said Jack. Seeing Joe DiMaggio make three hits and three spectacular catches left quite an impression on him too.

Jack won 5th place in the Junior Division class A gasoline powered free flight competition. His total time for three trips was 576 seconds. He helped Jerry Robertson, another contestant from his hometown, compete in the jet plane contest. Unfortunately, Jerry couldn't get his jet off the ground, even with Jack's help.

Later that same day, Jack chased his highflying Class A plane two miles before losing sight of it in a heavily wooded area. As he walked back, a civil aeronautics patrol plane dived low over his head and throttled down his engine. The pilot shouted to him that he had seen his plane come down and radioed its location to one of the search parties. The unidentified pilot wagged his wings in farewell and roared away to resume patrol duties.

That was fifty years ago, 1951. Jack flew with the eagles in the model airplane contest. He still has yellowed newspaper clippings telling his exciting story. If you ask him, he'll show you the ragged handkerchief that gave him the reputation of being the "hottest flier" in the International Model Airplane Contest.

* * *

Jack grew up, got a job and married me, Pat. His job was at Armour and Company, a nationwide meatpacking conglomerate with a large slaughtering plant in St. Joseph, Missouri. Built in 1898, plants like this operated before modern safety regulations were thought about and before OSHA became law.

In 1956 Jack was the maintenance engineer at the Armour plant in St. Joseph where they slaughtered 600 hogs per hour.

One day Stewart's job was to measure the hog dehairing machine for new shafts. The rubber beaters took off the hair from the dead hogs. He came in on a Saturday morning when the plant was shut down.

He crawled inside with his tape measure. All of a sudden the machine started up, slapping him like a hog. He dashed out and found Amos, the department mechanic. "Why did you start that machine with me in it?" Jack asked.

"I didn't know you were in there. Why didn't you lock out the machine?" asked Amos.

Jack learned a lesson that day. He bought his own lockout set and now, fifty years later, he still carries his own padlock and key on the job.

P.S. Jack didn't get dehaired that day, and at age seventy still has most of it!

* * *

The years have gone by. The seven children have grown up,

finished college and married. When Jack retired, I was not concerned that he would become the poster retiree golf nut. He had no interest in that pastime. He would be working part time at home. My main concern was the computer. I was accustomed to being able to use it from 8 A.M. till 5 P.M. anytime I wanted it. "Would it become a source of hassles?" I wondered.

Planning and schedules are Jack's passion. "I'll prepare a sign-up sheet. You sign up for your preferences, and I'll use it when you don't." That sounded good to a limited degree. The whole computer dilemma was solved when Jack needed a faster, glitzier computer. He got the new one: Windows 98, Pentium III, CD burner, more memory and faster everything. I was happy with his castoff: Windows 95, no burners or stuff to get screwed up. I use my old one whenever I want with no interference. For a while his fax didn't kick in so my old slow relic had to do for faxes until he figured out what was wrong with his fancy system.

We settled in to a life of comparative peace with his part-time teaching and my writing, grandchildren, and volunteer chores. I did have to head off his suggestion that he "organize your kitchen."

"What does that mean, organize my kitchen?" I asked.

"Don't you want your spices arranged alphabetically so you can find them easier? I could set up a program to inventory your canned food and you'd know when you need more eggs or beans."

"Thank you so much, but no thanks. I do well on my own. You can take that chore off your to-do list."

What really got his whole attention was a purchase he made last fall, a concrete mixer. "There are a lot of projects I can do with my own concrete mixer. First I want to make a sidewalk beside the house to the back yard."

And that's just what he did. He bought lumber for forms and spent weeks preparing the space for the concrete. It involved digging up huge tree roots and boulders left behind by the builders. Jack assessed every sidewalk we passed. "See how bad his finish is. He didn't have enough mortar." Or "He didn't float it like he should have. I'll do better than that."

Building a sidewalk of twelve sections four feet by four feet is a formidable project. After the prep work, Jack started making concrete. "Can I use your car today? I need to go to Home Depot to get concrete mix and rocks. That means I need to use the trailer. Do you mind?" This has come to be an almost daily routine. I barely use my old 1990 Camry with the trailer hitch. I get to use the 1996 Camry!

Making the sidewalk involved mixing 150 sixty-pound bags of concrete with 1,000 pounds of water. That's 10,000 pounds of wet concrete. Each bag of dry concrete meant lifting it three times, from Home Depot to car to mixer at home. Jack saw this as a way to develop "six-pack abs." That didn't happen.

He spent most of the fall digging, hauling, pouring and worrying once a concrete section was in. "If it gets too warm, it will harden too fast. If it rains, it will be ruined."

After the walk was completed, Jack pondered his next project. "I'm making a set of steps from the deck to the tomato patch."

"You have steps already," I protested.

"Those don't go close to my tomatoes. I want to be right there when I leave the deck."

This means a renewed affair with Home Depot. My car will be called into duty again. As Jack progressed on this home improvement,

I saw less and less of him and my Camry. "I need the trailer again today. Are you OK with that?"

We go over our day at breakfast. More and more I hear, "I'm going to Home Depot today." It is like it has become an addiction. I'm so glad it isn't alcohol or drugs. Or women. His forays out to Home Depot are legitimate. He never comes home reeking of beer or perfume. He comes home with a bag of screws, more lumber, and tomato food.

Next month the new steps will be ready and tomatoes will take over as the daily drill. Check the fertility of the soil, its temperature, find and assassinate any tomato cutworms. Most of the tomato equipment came from Home Depot. Maybe nurturing tomatoes will take over his days until frost. But I still expect several trips a week to Home Depot, just to see what's new out there.

* * *

Jack and I have settled into the retirement years. As we go forward in life, we have developed a routine of sorts. We refuse to be the geezers we see portrayed on TV ads. We joined the local YMCA and use its exercise machines, pool, and walking trail. Days we don't work out or swim, we walk the trail or a neighborhood route. We have children and grandchildren around and when they aren't here we visit them in states where they now live. We both have our own volunteer activities. Helping rebuild homes in Mississippi ravaged by the 2005 Hurricane Katrina is Jack's personal mission. I go along, not to hammer and saw, but to cook for the hungry laborers. It is a new way of life that enhances our lives now. We give back to the community and feel a sense of mission in our retirement years.

Opposites Attract

It was February nineteen hundred and fifty-five
That day when we joined together our lives;
Like other opposites who get married
It wasn't long till we saw how we varied.

I'm ready to get up long before dawn
As the sun rises, you slumber on;
Winter announces my very best times
While you long for hot and sunny climes.

Up North we braved snow and ice together
Kept up our work in all kinds of weather;
Now Southern pleasure suits you more
I like the mountains, you like the shore.

Your vacation beckons you to the beach
I head for the first mountains we can reach;
You dream of scads of bikini-clad kittens
I lust for overshoes and warm woolen mittens.

You grab the sports page and devour the scores
I go for the recipes and ignore those macho bores;
When we grab for the comics it's a sight to see
It's Dilbert for you and Blondie for me.

You love to coach children in ways of math
I'm doing good to read a simple graph;
"Dad, come help me with these fractions!"
"Mom, how do you spell attractions?"

Your day timer rules your days
My style runs to unplanned haze;
You want to arrive just barely on time
If I don't arrive early I think it's a crime.

We began as teenage sweethearts at the Valentine dance
Now a quiet evening at home is our romance;
Once we necked in a Studebaker on Wyeth Hill
Today lovemaking in our cozy home is a pleasure still.

About the Author

Patricia Webster Stewart was born in Missouri and graduated from Furman University. Her essays have appeared in magazines including *Woman's Day*, *Reunions*, and *Living with Teenagers*. Pat is a member of the South Carolina Writers Workshop (SCWW) in Greenville, SC. Her works appear in the SCWW Anthology in each of the past eight years, 2000-2007. The *Voices of Civil Rights* project, to be housed at the Library of Congress, featured her essay "Negroes into the Schools." Pat writes in Taylors, South Carolina and is a member of Mensa. Her seven children are grown. They and their children are still the subject of many of her stories.

Pat's second book, to be published in 2008, contains a collection of short stories from the tumultuous period from World War II to the present. Her provocative sense of humor helps the reader cope with the realities of today's world. On these pages you will find friends and lovers, church mice and the devil, Elvis Presley and George W. Bush. A special feature is her acclaimed article *How to Teach Your Teen to Drive*.